LEADING TEAMS

Understanding the Team Leadership Pyramid

STEVE GLADIS & KIMBERLY GLADIS

Dedication & Disclaimer

Dedication

To anyone who has ever led or will ever lead a team.

Disclaimer

Part I is a summary of the research, which is explained, in depth, in Part III.

Part II is a work of fiction. As such, names, characters, places, and incidents are products of the authors' imaginations or are used fictionally. Any resemblance to actual persons (living or dead), businesses, organizations, events, or locales is entirely coincidental.

Part III is a compilation of research on teams, which we offer to inform, motivate, and inspire leaders. It is presented with the understanding that neither we nor the publisher are engaged in rendering any type of psychological, legal, or any other kind of professional advice.

ISBN: 978-0-9891314-1-4 (paperback)

ISBN: 978-0-9891314-4-5 (e-book)

CONTENTS

INTRODUCTION

We both have spent years working in, working with, and leading teams. Steve has led combat teams in the Marine Corps, squads of Special Agents in the FBI, and departments at the University of Virginia. Kim has led teams in the Pharmaceutical & Biotech industries, and she has consulted for numerous sales, technical, and executive teams to help them work more effectively together. We both have researched and written about teams and team-related issues like coaching, onboarding, and positive leadership techniques. We currently coach a variety of corporate, government, and public service teams and are excited to share our findings and techniques with even more team leaders and organizations.

This book will be presented in three parts:

Part I: The Research Summary

This section summarizes comprehensive research, which will be further explained in Part III. This research is important grounding before reading The Story.

Part II: The Story

This section is a leadership fable, a fictionalized case study about how team leadership works in "real life." For years, we've been coaching and teaching leadership strategies and skills to corporate, government, and public service teams. While this story is a fable and the characters are entirely fictional, it's a collage of circumstances and experiences we've found in real-life teams. There is compelling research that supports using storytelling as an instructional and motivational tool. Storytelling aids memory, helps people make sense of complex information, and facilitates their passing along the story and teaching it to others. Further, the book and the story are written so that everyone in the company—from the stockroom to the boardroom—can read it and develop a common language within the company about its most important, organizational sustaining lifeblood: Teams.

Part III: The Research

This part of the book contains a compilation of current research on teams. While it isn't possible to capture all research, we believe that this summary will deeply ground the reader in the most up-to-date work done on teams and team assessment. Specifically, the extensive research at Harvard by Richard Hackman and Ruth Wageman on team conditions, which is at the core of team coaching and development of executive teams.

Part I

THE
RESEARCH
SUMMARY

Leading Teams:

Understanding the Team Leadership Pyramid

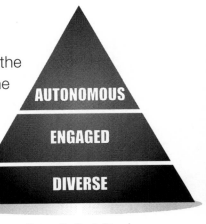

Figure 1 The Team Leadership Pyramid

Teams are the central focus of organizations, no matter whether you are discussing the military, nonprofits, or for-profit companies. Teams determine the success or failure of any organization. Indeed, most organizations are what retired General Stanley McChrystal calls a team of teams.[1] We have researched the researchers of teams to construct this practical model to help people develop high-functioning, competitive teams. Our model, The **Team Leadership Pyramid**, consists of 4 Elements: **People**, **Leader**, **Culture**, and **Strategy**. Moreover, extensive research at Harvard has produced 6 Conditions for team success, which reflect many of our findings, amplify their impact, and lay a solid, valid and reliable foundation for high performing teams.

PEOPLE

Talented people will be the name of the competitive corporate game for the foreseeable future. There are several reasons we can say that with conviction: Baby boomers are eligible to retire at staggering numbers—some estimates are 10,000 a day. Millennials are fast becoming the largest demographic in the workplace, and

Figure 2 The People Triangle

there aren't nearly enough of them to fill the vacancies of exiting boomers. Further, millennials are increasingly more interested in working in a gig-economy—like freelance consulting, working in an online startup, or even driving for Lyft or Uber to earn extra cash. The generation right behind millennials is called "digital natives."[2] They have grown up on the internet and have developed both a real and a digital identity, which will impact how, why, when, and where they choose to work. Therefore, leaders need to pay close attention to talent recruitment and retention because people matter—a lot. Our research of the researchers revealed that people on successful teams have three characteristics. They are diverse, engaged, and autonomous.

Diverse

People are different! Different is good when it comes to teams solving critical problems and coming up with new solutions, products, and services. While ethnic, gender, and cultural diversity are important to organizations that want to reflect their constituency, cognitive diversity is equally important. Steve Jobs constantly told the folks at Apple to "think different!" When team members think differently, they approach problems from alternative cognitive points of view, and they are collectively better able to solve complex problems.

Engaged

To keep people engaged, they must be interested in what they do and want to become excellent at it. Simply put, when people work toward their strengths rather than trying to "fix" weaknesses, they produce significantly better results. Character Strengths, assessed by using a well-researched and reliable tool developed out of the the University of Pennsylvania, helps reveal what truly inspires people—personal intrinsic values. Moreover, Cognitive Strengths, assessed by using a personality model, such as the Jungian model, helps identify people's thinking strengths—as either tactical or strategic thinkers. This provides teams with windows into how best to use their individual cognitive strengths—unique ways of thinking. When people get to use their best thinking styles every day at work, they become engaged and energized. Also, when all team members understand the way each other thinks, understanding and synergy can happen. Moreover, when used in tandem, Character Strengths and Cognitive Strengths are a potent combination that supercharges engagement at work.

Autonomous

Talented people and teams value autonomy. Independent thinking is a key intrinsic motivator for people. Autonomy is critical for team success. Unfortunately, vestiges of command-and-control leadership—anathema to autonomous thinking—still exist; however, over the past two decades, coaching has emerged as an increasingly dominant leadership model. Coaching focuses on and supports autonomous thinking. Research by Google in Project Oxygen, Dan Goleman in *Emotional Intelligence,* and others confirms the strength and effectiveness of the coaching model. By asking questions, leaders show respect, give status to their direct reports, and, at the same time, lead them to discover the answers to their own problems—the very definition of autonomy. The model that we've written about appears in *Leading Well: Becoming a Mindful Leader-Coach.* It follows the 4-Ps questioning model: 1. Problem: Ask questions to determine the real problem, not just the symptoms; 2. Present: Ask about the size, status, and impact of the present state; 3. Possible: Ask what is the ideal possible future state; and, 4. Plan: Ask for the first intentional steps you can take toward this future state.

LEADER

First, we need leaders. No leader, no team. Teams don't magically form or stay together without leadership. Groups can be mandated, but that doesn't mean they'll work like interdependent teams. Groups are gatherings of people who resemble kids in parallel play—each doing their own thing. They are only thinly connected, but neither align with nor take advantage of the team's diversity or experience. It takes

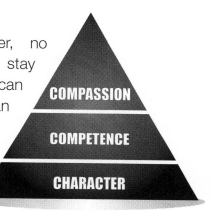

Figure 3 *The Leader Triangle*

leaders to turn groups into teams. The essence of leadership is trust. Without trust, leaders only possess positional authority. Without trust, one is a leader in name only. We've all seen this kind of positional leader in action, whose team members only do what's required and never go above and beyond. At best, untrusted leaders craft teams that only make incremental micro-progress—if any at all.

However, if you want team members who are "all-in" all the time, you need personal leadership—trust that comes from three places based on research: character, competence, and compassion.[3] Let's examine these three trusted-leader traits. First, character sits at the base of this pyramid because it's fundamental. If there is no respect for a leader's character, then leadership engagement is over.

Character

Trusted leaders possess the basic elements of good character—candor, communication, commitment, consistency, and courage.

- **Candor**—They are honest with themselves and others.

- **Communication**—They speak, write, and listen well.

- **Commitment**—They are dedicated to their teams and the organization.

- **Consistency**—They are stable, showing up the same way, day after day.

- **Courage**—They have the ability to speak truth to power when necessary.

Competence

People will follow a leader who has both personal and professional knowledge and experience. Great leaders 1) are self-aware, 2) understand and respect differences in others, and 3) know their profession. They know how to learn, adapt, and survive in their professions. They also know how to teach, coach, and mentor others.

Compassion

Finally, trusted leaders are compassionate. They are compassionate with themselves and others, not just feeling others' emotions but engaging with them. They're also compassionate with their companies, their communities, and their country. They care and do something about them all. They help, volunteer, run for office, and are the lifeblood of their communities.

CULTURE

Culture has been defined as "the way we do things around here"—the artifacts, symbols, and assumptions.[4] Think of it as an ecosystem. The support system consists of several critical elements—just like the sun, air, and water are critical elements of an ecosystem to grow plants. Leaders and people immersed in a culture (ecosystem) that is safe, connected, and purposeful make a difference in the organization. This model is derived from the work of famed psychologists Abraham Maslow and Frederick Herzberg.

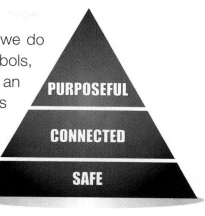

Figure 4 The Culture Triangle

Safe

At the triangle's base, safety relates to a state of mind that people, teams, and organizations require to produce the kind of innovative thinking that propels them forward in the marketplace of ideas, data, and leadership. When people are economically insecure, emotionally bullied, or hesitant to speak truth to power, their best thinking gets quashed, the truth gets drowned out, and people, teams, and organizations wither and become irrelevant.

Connected

After people feel psychologically safe and secure, they need to feel connected. By nature, humans are pack animals. Ever since humankind stopped being nomads, we settled down and established "place" as an important sociobiological concept.

Why? Because together in a place—a tribe, town, or city—we work together to support ourselves and to survive. When we moved onto farms, we needed each other to help harvest. When we hunted larger animals, we needed superiority of numbers to kill and eat animals that were stronger, larger, and faster than us. In short, we used our social brains to compete and survive in the world. Today is no different. We must stay connected to compete and survive in a global marketplace.

Purposeful

Meaning and purpose are conventionally joined at the hip. However, current research has identified distinctions. Meaning comes from doing what you do well and love to do. Purpose comes from doing what you love to do in service of the greater good—other people and society. Ultimately, we're all part of a community—sustained by and sustaining others. It does "take a village" to survive.

STRATEGY

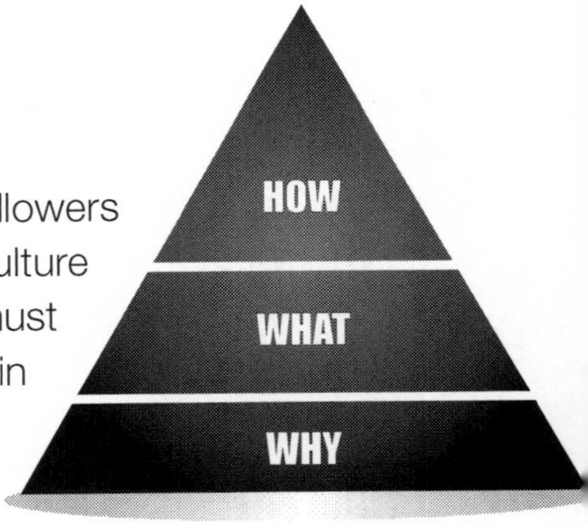

A great leader and engaged followers operating within an excellent culture are not quite enough. They all must be committed to rowing the boat in the same direction. This calls for a solid strategy, the rudder of the organizational ship. Strategy can become overly complex, as you might expect to see in larger organizations.

Figure 5 The Strategy Triangle

However, at a basic level, it boils down to three simple questions: why, what, and how.

Why?

Great strategies start with the simple question: Why? Three words answer this question: mission, vision, and values. Mission describes why the team exists. Mission is functional, rooted in action, and practical. Vision describes our aspirational future state. Where do we want to be in one to three years? If all goes well, what will we look like and how will we function? Values are fundamental moorings that we hold on to no matter how big we get. They're like the immune system of an organization. When they are compromised or corrupted, the organization gets sick and ceases to thrive.

What?

Once you know the "why"—mission, vision, and values— then you must get busy executing on the "what" that gets you there. That requires setting big goals that stretch rather than exhaust people. Often, people are too cautious when setting goals, leaving a good bit of their game on the practice field instead of playing to win. Former Stanford professor, researcher, and best-selling leadership guru Jim Collins talks about setting Big Hairy Audacious Goals (BHAGS).[5] The key is to think big because most of us think smaller than our capacity to perform. Each goal needs to support both the mission and especially the vision forward. Big vision, big goals.

How?

Goals point us in the right direction. Objectives get us to the destination. It's like a GPS—the broader city definition is entered first, followed by the street address to narrow in on the location. Goals are like the city settings and objectives are like the are like the turn-by-turn directions. To be effective, objectives need to be S.M.A.R.T. **(specific, measurable, achievable, relevant** and **time-bound)**. In other words, it's like giving someone specific directions to another person's house. In the best organizations, both goals and objectives cascade from the top down to every part of the organization. Everyone needs to be connected and accountable to the **mission, vision, values, goals,** and **objectives** of the organization.

THE 6 CONDITIONS

After decades of researching numerous teams in diverse industries, Richard Hackman, Ruth Wageman and others at Harvard discovered that as few as 20% of all teams are high performing. Based on this extensive research, they identified six conditions necessary for high performing teams, which we believe reflect components of the four elements (People, Leader, Culture, Strategy), amplify their impact, and lay a solid foundation for success. The six conditions include three essential and three enabling conditions that must exist for a team to be high performing.

The three essential conditions

1. Does a real team exist? Are they bounded (known to all), interdependent, and stable?

2. Does the team have the right people? Are they diverse and skilled enough—including teamwork skills—to meet the task challenge?

3. Does the team have a compelling purpose that is clear, challenging, and consequential?

The three enabling conditions

1. Does the team possess a sound structure to tackle problems? Teams need to have a solid task design, be the right size, and possess team behavioral norms.

2. Does the team have a solid support structure? Are there organizational structures and systems present that support and promote teamwork — like rewards and recognition, information, education, and resources?

3. Team Coaching: Is there a coach who is both available and helpful to the team and who intervenes at significant points during team interactions?

Based on their extensive team research, Hackman and Wageman developed the Team Diagnostic Survey (TDS™), which collects data from any team and assesses these six conditions. To date, the TDS™ is the most valid and reliable instrument of its kind in the world of teams. We describe it as being like an MRI of a team. It pinpoints foundational problems within a team that, if caught early on as it launches or relaunches, markedly increases its chances of becoming high performing.

Ensuring these six conditions are met is the foundation for the team's success. Together, they will impact the team task processes which will, in turn, drive the overall performance of the team.

Part II

THE CASE STUDY

Leading Teams:

Understanding the Team Leadership Pyramid

INTRODUCTION—
THE OGC CASE STUDY

Just as the *Harvard Business Review* uses fictional but realistic case examples to illustrate classic, complex, and relevant problems, our "case study" is also both fictional and realistic. Having coached leaders and teams over time, we believe that this example will help you visualize the principles we discuss in *Leading Teams.*

***

About five years ago, Drew Dillman retired from the federal government, where he worked in leadership development for the Office of Personnel Management (OPM). Tall, thin and muscular, Drew was a track star in college and kept himself in great shape over the years. An introvert by nature, Drew was thoughtful and careful with his words and actions. He learned it from his mother Estelle, a soft-spoken woman who taught him to listen first and then act. So, he was cautious when selecting from several good job offers from companies. He wanted to take advantage of both his federal experience and his doctorate in leadership and instruction from a local university, where he taught as an adjunct professor one night a week.

It was in that class where Drew met Harry Thurman, CEO of OGC, a government contracting firm in Virginia. Harry was a guest lecturer in Drew's organizational development class at the university. They struck up a conversation after one class, the first of many.

Harry told Drew about OGC and highlighted the rapid growth they had seen over the past 3 years. It was over 300 people strong with contracts in seven key government agencies. The prospect of further growth was high. Harry knew that, in such a tight job market, it would be hard to fill key first-line and mid-level executive positions if the company could not grow its own leaders. So, Harry made leadership development a strategic priority for the next three years. To make this happen, Harry knew he would need to invest substantially in leadership development.

That's where Drew came in. Over many post-class conversations, Harry collected information from Drew about his experiences at OPM, got to know Drew's leadership style, and probed him on his leadership development ideas. One evening, they met for dinner at Harry's favorite Vietnamese restaurant. At the end of dinner, Harry proposed, "So, Drew, I'd like you to come to work for OGC as the VP of Leadership & Organizational Development. What do you think?"

Intrigued, Drew asked Harry to share more specifics.

Harry explained that Drew would inherit three managers assigned to this new functional area. Harry also shared his vision for future leadership development and his willingness to put a budget in place before Drew came on board.

As Drew listened, he became excited about wanting to implement the best of his experience at OPM and his research at the university. To do this, he'd need to build a first-class team, knowing he'd want to follow a deliberate plan that was grounded in research. Over the past several months of discussion with Harry, Drew had done extensive research and had already developed a model he felt would help guide him in building a successful leadership development team.

When Harry finished describing the offer and context, Drew asked permission to share his ideas. Harry gave a thumbs up. Drew moved the plates to the side to reveal the rice-paper tablecloth and reached in his pocket for his favorite pen.

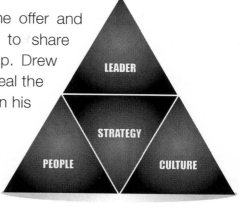

Drew sketched out his leadership development model focused on four critical elements: people, leader, culture and strategy. He told Harry how he developed the

Figure 6 The Team Leadership Pyramid

triangle from a combination of his experience at OPM and his coursework. He shared how he intended to use it as a model with this new team and that he felt it could be a good model for all the teams in the company. He and Harry discussed it for over an hour, only to discover they were the last ones in the restaurant, except for the waiter and maître d'. By the end of dinner, Drew was more than ready to join the OGC team.

THE OGC CASE STUDY

PEOPLE

A week before his start date, Drew had a long lunch with Harry to get a general understanding of the people on his new team and to gauge Harry's support for team growth. Harry told Drew that he was prepared to add a couple of people to Drew's team. And, if Drew had a compelling case and plan for others, Harry would be open to discussion.

Then, Harry provided background on each of the three current members Drew would inherit: Ralph, Maria, and Jonathan. Harry had high marks for all three team members. Ralph and Maria were excellent instructors who had been with the company for three years. Both were young and energetic. Ralph was from Boston and had been on an education content development consulting team prior to coming to Virginia to join the OGC team. Tall and shy, he was thoughtful—a lot like Drew—until he was in front of a group. Then Ralph lit up.

Maria was the team extravert. Originally from Puerto Rico, everyone described Maria as being "always on," entertaining, and a one-woman-show. After growing up in Providence, Rhode Island, she'd gone to the University of Massachusetts on an acting scholarship and had starred in several plays over her career. She'd even had a short stint on Broadway, but her uncle Sam was an entrepreneur and he always encouraged Maria to go into business. Maria interned with her uncle for two summers and enjoyed the corporate exposure. Sam recognized Maria's natural gifts of being able to command a room and her ability to engage with people. He thought she would be a good fit for a training role. He always joked with Maria saying, "Theater is fun, but training pays the bills."

Finally, there was Jonathan. Smart and highly educated in instructional design, he had been with the company the longest of the three. He was considered the linchpin to the team's future because of his technical skills in course and program design. In fact, he'd applied for Drew's job. He was very upset that his five years with the company, his education, and his performance had not earned him the job he so wanted.

***

Drew's first day in the office was busy and exciting. His first stop was a welcome meeting with Harry, and then HR. Then he was introduced to several peers, one of whom—Allison Pearson, Chief of Marketing—would act as Drew's mentor as he onboarded. Allison was slight and a bit shy, but she had a gentle smile that charmed everyone she met.

Drew immediately liked Allison and appreciated her calm advice. She would prove invaluable along the way. Never judgmental or critical of others, Allison acted more like a sounding board than an advisor. For example, when Drew asked her about his team and what she thought of them, she was supportive and positive. "I think it's a very strong team, and you'll come to make your own assessment of each of them and what you'll need going forward."

When Drew met the team later that morning, he formed initial impressions but kept those thoughts at a distance. He wanted to stay open to the group's potential. He immediately warmed to both Maria (who beamed) and to Ralph (who shook his hand with such force that he had to grip back strongly to avoid getting his hand crushed). However, Jonathan greeted Drew with a kind of half-smile—a neutral social recognition with no emotion, and the handshake was almost an afterthought.

For the first few weeks, Drew spent time asking questions and listening to his team members, his peers, and other key people at the company. He recorded thoughts and learnings in his trusty notebook—a constant companion for many years. His uncle gave Drew his first notebook when he was in high school. Drew kept one ever since. With everyone he met, he asked the same core questions: What did they do at the company? Where had they come from professionally? What did they think of his team? What advice did they have for him? He always closed each meeting by asking if they would be willing to periodically provide feedback on how he and his team were doing. These interviews yielded him a lot of great information and goodwill.

After the first month, Drew announced that he wanted to conduct a two-day offsite with his team. To prepare for that, he wanted each team member to take two online instruments:

- The VIA Character Strengths Survey, a tool that provided insight into what motivated people. https://www.viacharacter.org/

- The Jungian profiler, a tool that delivered a quick, directionally reliable personality profile. www.123Test.com

Drew explained that during the offsite, he would share the top character strengths for the entire team, including himself, and that the purpose was for the team to understand each member's complementary skills. Jonathan was the only one to push back on the request—saying that they already knew each other well and that two days out of the office would only put them further behind. Drew assured him it would be worth it.

Two weeks later at the team's offsite, Drew shared the results of the instruments and explained them, beginning with the VIA Character Strengths Survey.

Virtue	Character Strength				
	Team Members	Drew	Maria	Jon	Ralph
Wisdom	Creativity	13	18	12	17
	Curiosity	14	6	7	22
	Judgment	1	15	9	6
	Love of learning	19	23	11	7
	Perspective	18	17	19	4
Courage	Bravery	21	20	21	16
	Perseverance	16	22	4	14
	Honesty	3	12	1	3
	Zest	22	9	2	24
Humanity	Love	5	4	17	5
	Kindness	11	1	10	18
	Social intelligence	23	3	16	15
Justice	Teamwork	6	14	6	9
	Fairness	2	2	3	11
	Leadership	7	16	22	21
Temperance	Forgiveness	24	10	15	20
	Humility	17	19	20	10
	Prudence	12	5	5	19
	Self-regulation	4	24	24	23
Transcendence	Appreciates Beauty/excellence	20	21	23	1
	Gratitude	9	11	8	2
	Hope	10	7	13	12
	Humor	15	8	14	13
	Spirituality	8	13	18	8

Drew highlighted the top five values for each person and walked them through the six key virtue categories and twenty-four corresponding values. If people had two or more in one of the six virtue categories, he considered that category his/her superpower.

Maria jumped in, "You mean like the comics—Thor, Ironman, Wonder Woman—that kind of thing?"

"Kinda," Drew said, "but don't try jumping off any buildings just yet!"

Everyone but Jonathan laughed. Drew explained the results. He noted that he didn't have a superpower but was considered balanced as his results showed a spread over several virtues.

"So, you're a generalist," Jonathan said.

Drew nodded politely but continued. He explained that Maria's superpower was her humanity—how she related to people with love, kindness, and social intelligence. Altruistic acts of service for others, positive social behavior, and generosity of spirit were the hallmarks of this virtue.

Maria nodded and faked a seated bow to the crew.

Next, Drew focused on Ralph's superpower—transcendence. Drew noted that people who crave meaning and purpose in their lives possess this virtue. They seek connection to beliefs and goals bigger than themselves. The character strengths associated with transcendence are an appreciation of beauty, excellence, gratitude, hope, humor, and spirituality.

Finally, it was Jonathan's turn. Drew explained that Jonathan's superpower was courage—overcoming fear, either physical or psychological. Facing our fears doesn't demand a grand heroic effort. Rather, it's about facing the daily moments of bravery at home and at work. The character strengths associated with courage were bravery, perseverance, honesty, and zest.

Jonathan shrugged and said, "I think these kinds of tests are reductive and often invalid."

Drew paused. Then he said, "I'll send everyone the research on this particular instrument. It was developed at the University of Pennsylvania and has been validated by over 200 independent outside studies."

Jonathan glared but did not respond.

After some lively discussion and a break, everyone except Jonathan was abuzz and laughing. When they returned from the break, Drew explained that the Jungian assessment they took broke down personalities into four elements based on bipolar opposites: Extraversion vs. Introversion (where people get energy from); Sensing vs. Intuition (how they get information); Thinking vs. Feeling (how they make decisions based on the information), and finally, Judging vs. Perceiving (how they relate to the world).

Drew said, "Personality styles are often a series of four letters, like ESTJ or INFP. For the purposes of this discussion, we'll only consider a combination of the middle two elements of the Jungian assessment, known as the cognitive elements (how we think)— ST, SF, NF, NT." Then he explained each:

- STs are tactical thinkers. They are good with data and detail—the more the better. They tend to be linear, logical, and literal. They often find their way into data-based professions like engineering, analytics, and computer science. STs often end up leading teams and organizations.

- SFs are tactical feelers. They are not only good with data and detail, but also very good when working with people. They are the social glue that keeps teams together. They often end up in service-oriented careers like healthcare, teaching, and ministry.

- NFs are strategic feelers. They are big-picture oriented—more about new ideas and less about history and facts. They're also excellent when working with people and end up in jobs like teachers, ministers, and salespeople—communicating big ideas to people.

- NTs are strategic thinkers. They are big-picture oriented as well. NTs have a certain intellectual rigor about them. Interested in big ideas, NTs will attack problems using a rigorous, logically structured progression. NTs often end up leading teams and organizations. They are often doctors, lawyers, and college professors.

Then, Drew posted a flip chart in front of the room with each team member's personality type.

Ralph:	ISFJ
Maria:	ENFP
Jonathan:	ISTJ
Drew:	INTJ

"The good news is we are all different! Even better news is that these differences make for a great team," Drew exclaimed with energy. Then, he conducted several exercises with the team to show them how their personalities filtered how they took in information. For example, he asked them what they did on a perfect day. The three introverts spent lots of time reading, taking walks, or doing other singular tasks. But, the one extrovert,

Maria, liked to hang out with other people at the gym or at the coffee shop.

Drew noted that he'd keep both the values and cognitive styles flip charts posted up on the office wall for a few weeks to help people get to know each other even better. Drew said that he hoped that when new assignments came in, people could request them or even portions of assignments based on their strengths, making projects more collaborative and interdependent. For example, if a project came in that required team building, Maria might be the best lead. But she'd need structural help from Jonathan, who could also help make those often tough, courageous decisions.

Jonathan, who liked to have control, did not like the idea of interdependency. A heavy discussion ensued and ended with a strong commitment to accountability connected to interdependency. Moreover, Drew asked Jonathan to be the monitor of accountability, which elicited a slight smile—almost a smirk of satisfaction from Jonathan.

Drew then shifted to talking about his leadership style and explained that he was not an in-the-weeds micromanager—to which he got thumbs up and smiles from Ralph and Maria. Drew sketched a diagram on the wall showing the Coach-Approach model and explained that he would use it as he engaged with each team member and that the team would also use it to solve team problems. He gave them an article that he'd written on the topic, told them to read it for their next team meeting, and that they'd discuss it

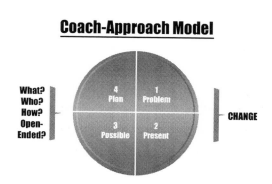

Coach-Approach Model

What?
Who?
How?
Open-
Ended?

4 Plan   1 Problem
3 Possible   2 Present

CHANGE

then. The model was based on autonomy—asking questions, not giving answers. Drew explained that this leadership model allowed people to make their own decisions and assumed that the person closest to the issue was more likely to make a better decision than a manager, who is at least one step removed from the situation.

Finally, Drew announced that he would be hiring two more people for the team to focus on content development, social media, online training, and development. The meeting ended with everyone talking about two takeaways they'd gotten from the meeting. Even Jonathan responded with a bit of positivity.

Progress, Drew thought.

THE OGC CASE STUDY

LEADER

Two weeks after the team retreat, Drew was getting settled in and more comfortable with the team dynamics. He felt like each of them now had a sense of what motivated everyone on the team and of their individual personality styles.

Drew started to unpack some boxes he'd brought in. One was a small eight-inch bust of Aristotle that he put on the corner of his desk. Then, he started to hang pictures around his office—a few watercolors of the ocean where he loved to spend his summers, and a few

family pictures placed on his desk and on his bookshelf to keep his focus on what mattered most to him—family. Finally, he put up a framed sign composed of four words.

A few days later, he brought the sign to a staff meeting. He started the meeting explaining his love of Aristotle, the famed thinker and Greek philosopher. "If I ever coached a dream team in the Olympics of Thought, Aristotle would be my point guard—the playmaker!"

Maria blurted out, "Where would LeBron fit in?"

"On ANY basketball team ever!" replied Jonathan.

"Agreed," said Drew, "But, this team is for great thinkers like DaVinci, Einstein, and Socrates. Thinkers like that."

Drew recalled that his favorite class as an undergraduate was Rhetoric, where they studied Aristotle—the Father of Philosophy—who wrote on such topics as poetry, physics, biology, linguistics, psychology, theater, rhetoric, and much more. When learning about rhetoric in Speech 100 at A local university, Drew learned about how speakers influenced other's thoughts and ideas—through ethos, the speaker's reputation; logos, data; and pathos, emotion. Of these three, ethos was most important because it all boiled down to this question: Can I trust that this speaker is telling me the truth? Aristotle described trust as good character, good sense, and good will. All of which translated to the 3-Cs: character, competence, compassion—what Drew called the Trust Triangle.

"I ask everyone I work with to hold on to one key value: Trust. If we have that one value on our team, nothing will get in our way."

Then, he proposed an exercise where they all wrote down three words associated with each of the 3-Cs. As each of them commented, he captured their thoughts on the flip chart and came up with the following list they could all agree to:

Character—honesty; consistency; truth; say and do; don't lie, cheat or steal

Competence—skills; wisdom; know the job; reliable; first-rate

Compassion—caring; empathy; sympathy; helping

The team discussed the findings. Then Drew asked, "Can you recall a time when, here at work, people exhibited the 3-Cs? Take a moment and write some notes. "

"OK, any thoughts you're willing to share?" Drew asked.

Maria spoke first, like always, and talked about one program manager who refused to take credit for writing a winning proposal—even though he had a great deal to do with winning it. Instead, he pushed all the credit onto his team.

"What was the result of that behavior?"

"Everyone wanted to work for that guy until he retired."

But, then, Jonathan piped up, "I've seen it go the other way too. We used to have a programmer who would literally steal ideas and code from others on the team and claim they were his work. He was an instant hit with management—he sucked up well."

"OK, and what happened to him?"

"Eventually, his team ratted him out and rejected him like a bad virus. He left."

"Both great examples of what happens when you have good character or bad character."

Everyone smiled, except Jonathan.

Drew shifted gears, "How about examples of competence?"

Ralph raised his hand and spoke, "I remember when Harry hired his wife's cousin to join the proposal team."

Ralph explained that the cousin was an English teacher and he'd been laid off. So, Harry wanted to help him out and figured he'd be a great fit to write and edit proposals. He was a disaster—had no idea about how proposals worked, acted like an elite know-it-all, and nit-picked the language to death.

"A colossal incompetent, pain-in-the-neck."

Maria piped up, "Ditto!"

Jonathan agreed as well but stared right at Drew and added: "We see this a lot. Harry falls in love with someone he meets or wants to help someone out, and we get stuck with the fallout—their incompetence. It's not fair to the rest of us who've been good soldiers for years."

"I see," Drew said as he stared back at Jonathan. Maria and Ralph shifted uncomfortably in their chairs.

Finally, Drew said, "Let's talk about compassion." He explained briefly that compassion was caring, only supercharged. It was more about alleviating the pain of another, not just feeling sympathy or empathy for another's distress.

Maria's hand went up like a rocket. "We had a guy, Jim, whose wife got really sick. Jim worked on a contract with the Marine Corps out of Quantico, but he needed time to take care of his wife. Harry and two other guys rotated onto the contract with permission of the Marines so Jim could work on another project remotely for six months until she recovered. No one will ever forget the compassion that Harry showed to keep Jim on the payroll and ensure health care coverage."

Both Ralph and Jonathan agreed that was the best example either of them could remember.

"Great story, Maria. Thanks. Personally, I've always found Harry to be a compassionate guy who is willing to step in or step up."

They had more discussion, and, at the end of the meeting, Drew asked Jonathan to hang back. When Maria and Ralph left the room, Drew turned to Jonathan and said, "Jonathan, when you discussed Harry's cousin and how Harry 'fell in love' with people and the team got stuck with the fallout, I felt like the comment was directed at me. Is that accurate?"

At first, Jonathan shrugged it off and denied it, but Drew kept pushing him. Finally, Jonathan burst out, "Damned right. I've been here for years, and you walked in and stole my opportunity."

"Stole it?"

"I should've gotten the job, but Harry met you—another shiny object for him—and I got pushed down again. It was more than discouraging, and I…"

Drew thought for a minute and then said, "Believe me, I get your frustration. So now we've got to figure out what would make you happy."

"Not sure anything would at this point."

"Look, I can't have you feeling discouraged, you're too valuable to this team. How about if we give it a few days? Then, maybe you, Harry, and I can sit down to talk about what could be next for you and plan a path toward that."

Jonathan nodded, "OK."

THE OGC CASE STUDY

CULTURE

Drew wanted to get started on building his leadership team, as he and Harry had discussed. So, he raised it early in his team meeting to get some thoughts. The first round of discussion centered on skills—what the team needed to develop and deliver leadership programs—both for first-line managers and for high potential future executives.

Both Maria and Ralph thought the team had enough trainers. They thought they could handle the new programs along with other training they were already conducting, like presentations, team management, and conflict skills. Jonathan also thought he could handle any new program development as well.

Drew agreed that everyone was doing a great job and could likely handle the expansion. But he also knew that starting new programs took much more effort than sustaining old ones. He also knew that Jonathan was a bit of a flight risk since he was clearly unhappy about not being promoted.

Drew announced to the team, "I hear you all but, at the same time, I think we need to over-staff to get these programs up and running. So, to get started, I'd like to hire a junior educational content developer—preferably someone with leadership development experience. That person would report directly to Jonathan, who will serve as a mentor." Jonathan cracked a slight, cautious smile.

Drew then explained that he also wanted to hire a digital manager for the online components of the curriculum. Maria jumped in, "But, we've always been an in-person training house."

Drew replied, "And we'll still be doing that. Also, as we grow and get more distributed, we'll need an online, digital platform to reach clients across all locations and time zones." Both Maria and Ralph reluctantly nodded and agreed that it made sense.

"OK, I want the three of you to be on the interview committee with me. I'll ask HR to get started on recruitment, and we'll look to start interviews in about four to six weeks."

When that meeting was over, Drew scheduled time with Harry to discuss corporate culture—especially because he'd be bringing two new people into the tribe.

Harry's office was open, comfortable, and transparent—lots of windows. Harry gestured for Drew to sit in one of the two large leather chairs in a conversation area off to the side of his desk, which looked like a door that sat on two file cabinets. Drew commented that it looked like a door. Harry said, "You're right. When I started this company in my garage, this was my desk. It's a constant reminder. Keeps me humble." Drew nodded and gave him a thumbs up. Harry had just confirmed one of the key reasons Drew had taken the job with OGC—Harry.

"So, you wanted to discuss culture?"

Drew nodded and said, "Look, I've read about OGC's culture and seen the logo all over the place: *Safe-Connected-Purposeful*. I love it and intend to use it with my team but wanted to ask a question or two about it."

"Shoot," Harry said.

"OK, how did you derive it?"

Harry talked about his executive coach, JC Williams—a legend in DC and Northern Virginia. JC helped him design and build the company—including setting up the mission, vision, values, goals, and objectives.

"In your interview process, we touched on mission, vision, and values. So, let me talk about our culture triangle," Harry said as he pulled out a piece of paper with a diagram of the triangle on it. He explained how JC spent a lot of time with the original corporate team way back when they started.

Harry and Drew talked for about an hour, and when they concluded, Drew was sold on Harry's culture triangle. Time to make it relevant to his crew.

One afternoon, Drew scheduled an extended team meeting, the purpose of which was to apply the company's culture model to their leadership development team. To start the meeting, he sketched out a big triangle on the flip chart in the front of the room. Next, he wrote out the word "Safe." Then he asked, "Please take a few minutes and think about any job you've had where you felt safe to speak truth to power. For example, you felt free to disagree openly with your boss and you weren't afraid of being reprimanded. Then, jot down what made you feel safe in that job."

Following about a five-minute break, he asked what people had written.

Maria said she felt safe when she went to work for her uncle's landscaping business. She explained that her uncle had a perpetual smile and always asked, "How can we do it better?" Her uncle set the tone from day one. Maria remembered the first time she suggested re-evaluating the crew schedules based on something she'd read. Instead of defending the old way, puffing up his chest, and bragging about his twenty-five years of experience in landscaping, her uncle was curious, asked for the website, and thanked Maria. After he'd checked out the website, her uncle decided to experiment with the new process. Ultimately, he found that the new scheduling approach served customers more effectively and resulted in much happier staff.

Jonathan mentioned a professor in graduate school, who not only encouraged debate as a way of finding finding truth, but also designated a "devil's advocate" in every class. The role of this individual was to question what was being taught to make sure people felt safe to disagree.

Ralph mentioned his former basketball coach, Coach T, who was always looking for a new defense or offensive system that was better. "He would try anything, no matter how wacky— AND he'd already won five state titles in his career!"

Drew took notes on the flip chart and then moved on to the next word: Connected.

"So, moving up the triangle, describe a team that you've been on in the past where you felt connected and how that happened."

Following another five-minute session by themselves, Drew asked, "OK, what did you come up with?"

Ralph led off the discussion and talked about his first day at a new high school. He'd just moved into the neighborhood and didn't know anyone. He participated in the high school basketball team tryouts and was excited when he made the team. But he was also nervous since he didn't know any of the other players yet. On the first day of practice, Coach T didn't start out on the court like most other teams Ralph had been on. Instead, he had the team do some 'get to know each other' exercises and he shared the reasons he selected each player, so everyone knew how best to leverage each other's talents. By the end of practice, everyone was laughing and had a respect for what each of them brought to the team. Throughout the season, Coach T set up regular team interactions off the court to make sure the players also connected personally. The more the team connected, the better they played.

Jonathan, who was now more animated, mentioned how his best friend used to build telescopes with science kits. One day, he invited Jonathan to join him, which led to Jonathan joining a group of telescope nerds called the Long Eyes. "We were geeks and proud of it!"

Finally, Maria mentioned her start at OGC. Harry spent over an hour with her and assigned Maria a mentor—a senior guy on another team—to teach her the ropes. It made such a difference. Almost immediately, Maria felt accepted and connected to the group.

Again, Drew put notes up on the flip chart. Finally, Drew mentioned purpose and meaning. He asked, "Where in your life, on a team, did you feel a sense of purpose and meaning? What was your gift to others?"

After five minutes of thinking time, Maria popped her hand up first. She told a story about her eleventh-grade history class. It was a tough group of students and many of them were struggling. Maria noticed this and started to interject some humor and provide encouragement to the group. One day after class, her teacher Mr. Zoltan asked her to hang back. At first, she thought she was in trouble but was pleasantly surprised when he thanked her for helping to boost the energy and morale in the room. He said she made the class lighter, more fun and, as a result, everyone was more engaged. "So, my role, I think, is to be a team morale booster!" Maria said with a big smile.

Drew smiled as he wrote 'morale booster' on the chart.

Then Jonathan spoke up, "When my cousin started his plumbing business, he had no sense of process—he did things by the seat of his pants. And he was good." But, as Jonathan explained, when the business grew, he found what worked for him in the beginning no longer worked. "So, I helped him map out more efficient and effective processes to support the evolved business model and he called me 'The Process Kid.' I think that's the gift I bring."

"I love it," Drew said as he put those words on the chart.

Finally, Ralph mentioned being able to simplify complex material. When he was in college and people got confused in a class, they'd inevitably come by his dorm room and explain the problem. He would ask a bunch of questions and then say, "Well, it sounds to me that…." When he said those words, people who knew him well realized it was time to take notes. He finished by saying, "They used to call me 'The Simplifier'."

"Great, Mr. Simplifier," Drew said.

Then, Jonathan spoke up, "Hey Drew, how about you? What's your gift?"

Drew thought and mused, "Hmm…my gift. I love to coach people and watch them get better at whatever they're already good at. I really enjoy helping people develop and seeing them grow."

Maria interjected, "Drew, I think we might have a new name for you, 'The Developer'!" Everyone laughed and Drew added The Developer to the list in front of them.

After looking at his watch, Drew said, "We've been at this a while. To summarize, Maria is the morale booster, Jonathan is the process kid, Ralph is the simplifier and I'm the developer. Also, we've all seen how each of us as a team and individually can fit within the corporate culture triangle: safe, connected & purposeful. Next week, we'll look at Strategy, and then we'll be ready to shift into high gear."

THE OGC CASE STUDY

STRATEGY

Drew hired JC Williams, an executive and team coach, to conduct what JC called a team relaunch, which is used to either launch a new team or reset an existing team. Two weeks before the meeting, JC sent out the Team Diagnostic Survey (TDS™), a validated and reliable team assessment developed at Harvard. The survey measured three essential and three enabling conditions of a team which make up ~80% of the team's foundational success. These conditions then influence three process areas—effort, knowledge, and strategy—which, in turn, drive three reliable success metrics—member satisfaction, quality of group process, and task performance.

When JC got the results, he sat down with Drew and discussed them at length. The good news was that the team seemed engaged. The team rated high in two essential conditions— right team, right people, and lower in the third area—compelling purpose. Second, in the enabling conditions, again they rated two high—supportive context and sound structure, but one lower—team coaching. When it came to rating the key task processes, the team rated effort and knowledge high but strategy lower. Finally, when they rated team effectiveness, they rated member satisfaction and task performance high but quality of group process lower.

"My read on this report is that you have a healthy, engaged team that could benefit from a more compelling purpose to shore up the essential conditions, the very foundation of a successful team. Additionally, it is important for the team to have coaching more readily available and the coaching must be helpful. These are the two most important areas to address first. If you get these in good condition, they will drive the team key task processes.

The team will benefit by developing a clear strategy so everyone is aligned on what the team is trying to achieve and how they will achieve it. Once those components have been addressed and are working, the team could benefit from a conversation later about how the team is working together and what they feel is needed to improve that process."

Drew agreed with JC's assessment. Since the group did not require a lot of prework, as indicated by the assessment, JC scheduled the relaunch meeting.

***

Two weeks later, the team convened at a meeting space close to the office. JC felt it was important to get the group out of their daily environment and provide them with a place to be focused and engaged on the team and not distracted by day-to-day work. Drew kicked off the team relaunch meeting with a few opening comments. Then, JC conducted a couple of opening exercises to loosen up the group. The best one was to tell something funny or odd about themselves that their colleagues might not know. Turns out, Jonathan had worked in high school as a clown for kids' parties. Ralph was a champion fly caster. Maria played the accordion as a kid. And Drew had been a chess champ when he was ten. They were all amazed at the diversity of skills and interests across the team. This was a great start to the meeting and put people at ease and in a positive state of mind.

Next, JC revealed three flip charts for all to see how the day would unfold:

- Team Purpose

- Team Strategy

- Introduction to Team Coaching

He said, "We'll need to answer all these questions for your team":

Why?

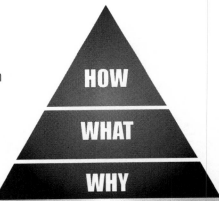

- Mission: Why does this team exist? What is its purpose?

- Vision: What does this team aspire to become or deliver in the future?

- Values: What values or principles will be the guiding lights/north-star principles for this team?

- Working Agreements: What are acceptable team behaviors and norms? How do we agree to treat ourselves?

What?

- Goals: What are the interdependent goals—results—the team needs to achieve?

- How do they relate directly back to the Why?

How?

- Objectives: How do we get there? What steps do we need to take to achieve those goals?

- Measures: How do we measure whether we have accomplished the objectives? Think S. M. A. R. T. Specific. Measurable. Attainable. Relevant. Timebound.

The session lasted about four hours with a few breaks in between and entailed a lot of give and take. JC facilitated friendly debate, and he also captured long-winded issues on a flip chart off to the side titled 'Parking Lot' to keep the team from going off-topic. He focused the group on their two major goals—developing both a first-line leader and a high potential leadership program. The team worked to map out exactly how and when they would get things done. After much discussion, JC mapped out what would essentially become a monthly scorecard for the team to measure progress and created a 1-page document the team could refer to regularly—the Team Charter.

OGC Leadership Development Team Charter

The Why:

- **Mission**: Our team exists to develop, deliver, and evaluate high-performance leadership development programs for OGC—specifically for both first-line and high potential leaders.
- **Vision**: To be considered the gold standard for our focus on leadership development in government contracting by an outside assessor—like the Association for Talent Development (ATD) or the Society for Human Resource Management (SHRM).
- **Values**: Transparency, Collaboration, Trust
- **Working Agreements**:
  - Be present (cell phones off and away unless needed for an exercise)
  - Fight fair (no name-calling or ganging up on anyone)
  - Bring your A-Game (come to meetings prepared)
  - Protect the team (when you leave a meeting, no bad-mouthing anyone)

The What:

- Develop a 6-month training curriculum for first-line managers by July 1, and
- Develop a 1-year training curriculum for high potential leaders by October 1

The How:

Goals and Objectives

	GOALS	MEASURE(S)
1	**Develop a 6-month training curriculum for first-line managers by July 1**	• Conduct research on existing programs from similar organizations by February 15 • Complete an internal competency assessment for first-line leaders by March 31 • Develop and test curriculum by June 15 • Senior management review and approval by July 1
2	**Develop a 1-year training curriculum for high potential leaders by October 1**	• Identify core competency elements in discussion with senior leadership by February 1 • Evaluate off-the-shelf content options and consultant resources by March 1 • Identify subject matter experts for key topics by April 15 • Each subject matter expert to work with existing content and consultant resources to develop training module and workbook by September 1 • Review curriculum and training plan with Executive Committee by October 1

After the team charter/strategy was completed, JC introduced the team to the concept and importance of Team Coaching.

"Team Coaching is considered an important enabler of a team's success. It requires someone play the role of a coach for the team—that person can be the team leader, a team member, or even an external coach like me. The coach needs to be available to the team, to look at the team's processes, and to intervene at helpful moments. What we found in the report is that when coaching is available, it is often very helpful. However, it appears it may not be as available as it needs to be. Drew has committed to engaging me for the next twelve months to work with your team in this capacity. We will meet monthly as a team for three-hour sessions where I will take you through two components. We will spend the first hour checking in on progress, adherence to and/or adjustment of the charter. During the second part of the meeting, we will focus on team problem-solving. I will teach you guys the 'Coach-Approach' to problem-solving. We will use this model at each session. Once you get familiar with it, you will be able to use this model during the regular course of business to help each other work through problems. Our first meeting is next month, and I am looking forward to getting started!"

Drew and the team all nodded in agreement and shared their excitement about having such a great resource available to help them. At the end of that day, JC complimented the now tired group for doing such a great job.

The Team Problem Solving Process

A month later, at the first follow-up team meeting after the relaunch, JC began the session by reviewing the charter. He reviewed the commitments and probed the team on progress towards each of the objectives. In the conversation, they adjusted the action steps or the due dates as needed. JC ensured that ownership was assigned to all tasks, so it was clear to the entire team and everyone was held accountable.

During the second half of the follow-up meeting, JC introduced the team to the 'Coach-Approach Model.' He drew it on the whiteboard at the front of the room.

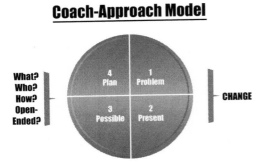

Coach-Approach Model

JC pointed to the problem-solving section of the section of the model by saying:

"OK, I want you each to consider the top one or two problems that you think your team will face in the near-term future. Problems that might impede your ability to reach your goals. Write them down, and when you finish, discuss them amongst yourselves."

Ten minutes later, JC called on the group to surface a couple of key issues. They suggested that beyond recruiting new help for their own development team, recruiting the high potentials' cohort would be a difficult process. They agreed that the high potential cohort issue was worth starting to focus on.

JC wrote on the flip chart: *Recruiting the cohort for high potentials.* Next, he reviewed the rules for the team Coach-Approach process:

- Only questions are allowed. Participants can only make a statement in response to a direct question.

- Anyone could ask anyone a question.

- JC controlled the group and could stop and start it anytime he needed to.

Everyone agreed and JC pointed to the Coach-Approach Model on the wall. Specifically, he pointed to the Problem quadrant. "There is a great Albert Einstein quote I like to reference before we begin. Einstein said, 'If I had an hour to solve a problem, I'd spend fifty-five minutes thinking about the problem and five minutes thinking about solutions.' He understood the importance of clearly defining the problem. So, who has the first question about the problem?"

Maria spoke first.

"I think that the senior executive team..."

JC cut her off, "What's your question, Maria?"

There was an awkward silence, and Maria just shrugged.

"OK, who has a question about the problem?"

Jonathan spoke up, "My question is: How do we define the term 'high potential'?"

Drew answered, "If I can respond to that question, I would say someone who is next in line for a larger leadership role, someone the organization is investing in to develop and groom for more responsibility."

Ralph nodded.

JC stopped the process and asked, "Does everyone agree with Drew? Any reasons not to?" The entire team discussed the definition but, eventually, came back to agreement with that statement.

"I have a question for the group," JC said. "Would the executive leadership team say the same thing? Would they agree with that definition?"

Everyone looked around, realizing they didn't know the answer to that question.

Then, Drew said, "I guess the problem really is how do we, as a company, go about defining a 'high potential'?"

JC paraphrased the discussion when he wrote the statement on the flip chart. It said, "Do we all agree now that how the company defines 'high potential' is really the current problem as we start down this training road?"

Unanimously, everyone nodded or said yes aloud.

JC moved onto the next quadrant: Present. He asked the team, "What is the present state of how 'high potential' is defined? What happens if this group defines 'high potential' and starts developing the program?"

Jonathan answered," I think it would be faster if we defined it ourselves. But, that's risky, especially if the senior execs felt they weren't offered the opportunity to share their perspective."

After some discussion, there was unanimous agreement that the execs would need to be engaged in defining high potential for the organization or the development team could make some big initial missteps.

JC nodded. Then he pointed to the next quadrant: Possible. He asked, "OK, so, what does the possible future state look like?"

Maria said, "I think the possible future state is where we, as a team, have done some initial work to map out what we think the definition of 'high potential' could be at OGC. Then, we would share our recommendation to the exec team to provide them with a starting point and solicit their feedback to finalize the definition. Once we have that definition, we can move to the next stage of understanding the competencies needed for this group to help us develop a successful curriculum."

"How does that sound to everybody?" JC asked.

All heads nodded in agreement.

Then JC pointed to the last quadrant: Plan. He asked, "What are the first few steps that the team should take and who will do what?"

Jonathan spoke up, "For the first step of coming up with our recommendation, would it help if we reached out to our contacts to see what definitions other companies are using as a starting point?"

"Good idea," Drew said.

After some discussion, they decided that the team would make a list of contacts at other companies that they could reach out to reach out to learn how their organizations define high potentials and what process they used to arrive at that definition. Each person signed up to reach out to three contacts before the next team meeting. Ralph also said that he would contact ATD and SHRM for some competency standards. Maria said she'd review the academic research to find definitions that might be helpful. While those calls were underway, Jonathan offered to work with Drew to build a questionnaire for the execs. They would share it with the team at the next meeting. Finally, they agreed to meet again with JC in a month to report back on their progress.

After recording the assignments on a fresh sheet of flip chart paper, JC smiled and gave a thumbs up. They agreed on the next meeting date.

Finally, JC asked the group to write one or two things that were of value to each of them personally. After a couple of minutes of quiet time, JC said, "Let's start with you Maria."

Maria was ready and willing, "I liked the bagels!" Everyone laughed, and then she added, "Really, I like how the charter keeps us on track."

Then, Ralph spoke, "I learned the value of taking time to really figure out what the problem is."

Next, Jonathan said, "I like the idea of getting much more information before talking to senior management."

Drew spoke last. He said, "I like how we've come together as a team."

"Great, and on that note, have a great month," JC said.

***

EPILOGUE

Two years have gone by and much has happened at OGC. Most notably, the company has seen a significant revenue increase and organizational growth. As far as the team's accomplishments, they include the following:

- After the team successfully delivered the first-line and high potential leadership development programs, the organization was able to promote five employees to next level positions.

- Maria was promoted to Master Trainer and has hired her own staff of three people. Jonathan continued to develop and demonstrate his leadership skills, so much so that Drew gave him additional responsibilities that fulfilled Jonathan's desire for growth and development.

After working with the team for two years, JC measured the team itself based on reliable and valid evaluation research from Harvard. He used three criteria developed by researchers:

- **Task Performance,** which measures if the team did what its clients required. This includes the quality, quantity, and timeliness of deliverables. In this team's case, they delivered the following on budget and on time, just as they committed to in their original team charter:

  - A first-line manager program that was very successful. It even had a waiting list to attend the next session.

- A high potential leader program, which not only identified future execs but also had a high retention rate of those in the program.

- **Quality of Team Process,** which measures how well the team performed as an interdependent team over a series of projects.

  - JC asked each of the team members to rate the team's overall effectiveness. He asked, "Did the entire team get better at working in unison on major projects?" On a scale from 1-5 (1 was low and 5 was a high rating), the team average was 4.65—a very respectable number.

  - JC also collected comments like "It took a few months, but then we jelled into a solid crew." And "We had to get used to our differences and see them as strengths."

- **Member Satisfaction,** which measures how much the team contributed to the learning, growth, and satisfaction of each team member.

  - Again, JC rated each person on a 1-5 scale. The average was 4.5.

  - Comments focused on personal growth and struggles. Not just with the other team members, but also on their own personal development. One member wrote: "It felt great to be part of a team that really mattered." Overall, they each expressed that they had grown in a positive direction and would sign on with this team again—the real final test of team effectiveness.

Part III

THE
RESEARCH

Leading Teams:

Understanding the Team Leadership Pyramid

01: INTRODUCING THE TEAM LEADERSHIP PYRAMID

Understanding and employing how teams work effectively can make the difference between average and great companies. Why? Because fast-moving global economies demand it. Think about it. When we lived on farms in small villages, the competition was local, minimal, unsophisticated, and often unhurried. Small-town politics, established brands, and strong clans kept competition down and the establishment in place. However, when people moved to towns, cities, to new states, and even to new countries, competition expanded. We went from a local to a global village, and competition intensified.

At the same time, technology exploded. Look at how many industries have been disrupted because of technology. Today, Uber, the largest transportation company, owns no cars; the largest retailer, Amazon, owns few brick and mortar storefronts; and, Airbnb, the largest online lodging company, owns no hotels. Scalability is all about the internet and the network—adapting, innovating, and scaling-up companies quickly.

In today's economy, failing to be adaptive and innovative is the kiss of death because companies must compete in a fast-moving global economy. Teams are at the center of innovation. Groups of diverse people are bounded by interdependent goals and work together to find solutions and develop new products and services. Why? Because when teams don't work well together, bad things happen, and businesses falter and die.

As we move with ever-accelerating technological speed toward a globally, hyperconnected world, the changes will happen even faster, and teams will need to respond because, as the research tells us, cognitively diverse teams comprised of people focused on a task are more innovative. Teams, not merely groups, are the critical element of change in any organization.

TEAMS VS. GROUPS

All of us have been members of a group. Groups share a common goal. For example, in college, you may have been a student in a history or business class and engaged in a study group. We all want to get the basic concepts of history or business down and pass the course, and while we may help each other along the way, my grade is not dependent on you.

Groups and teams are two very different things, and if we're lucky, we've had the privilege of being on a real team. For example, you might have been on an athletic team at some point. What you do or don't do greatly affects me. If you refuse to pass to me when I'm open on the field or court, it greatly affects the team. In business, a project team tasked with delivering a new innovative solution requires each team member to play his/her part for the overall project to be successful.

So, what's the difference between teams and groups? Teams have shared purposeful and interdependent goals. After decades of research at Harvard, Richard Hackman and Ruth Wageman determined that high performing teams have stability, clear boundaries, defined membership, and strong interdependent goals.[6]

Healthy organizations are collections of high-performing, well-integrated teams that support organizational goals and objectives. Thus, teams are at the core of a strong organizational leadership model. To build a high performing team, it takes four critical elements: **people, leader**, **culture**, and **strategy**. This book will guide you through each of those four critical elements of successful teams by offering simple, powerful rules based on research—simplicity based on complexity. We call this model The Team Leadership Pyramid.

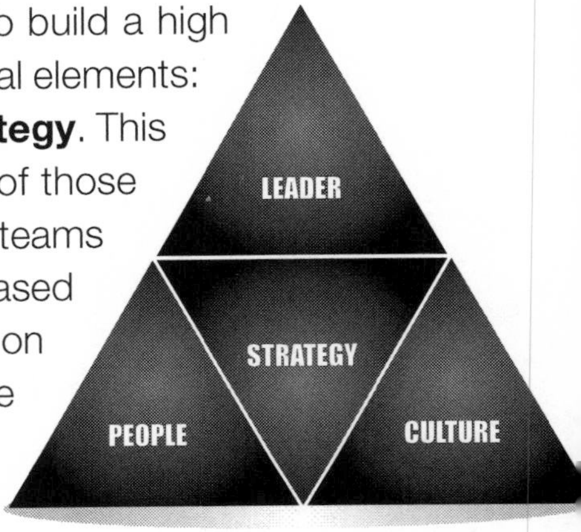

Figure 7 The Team Leadership Pyramid

02: PEOPLE

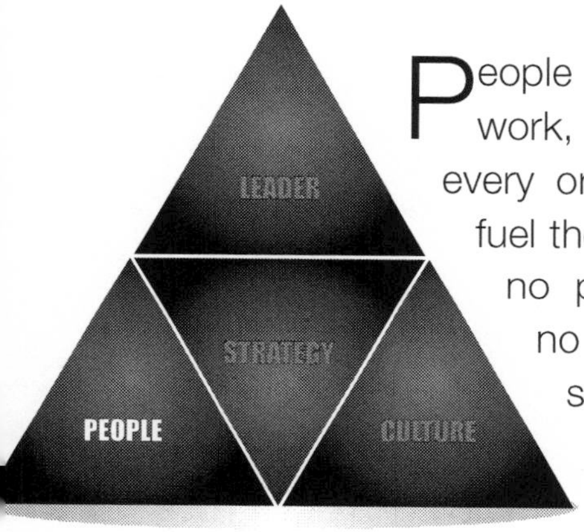

Figure 8 The Team Leadership Pyramid: People

People fuel the economy: No people, no work, no economy. The same is true for every organization—large or small. People fuel the organization: No people, no work, no products or services, no revenue, no company. Further, considering the shifting demographics like nearly 10,000 baby boomers a day become eligible to retire, talent—people with necessary skills—has become an increasingly precious commodity.[7]

When it comes to people working in concert to solve difficult problems, research has proven that three key elements get to the heart of the matter. People must be: **diverse, engaged** and **autonomous.**

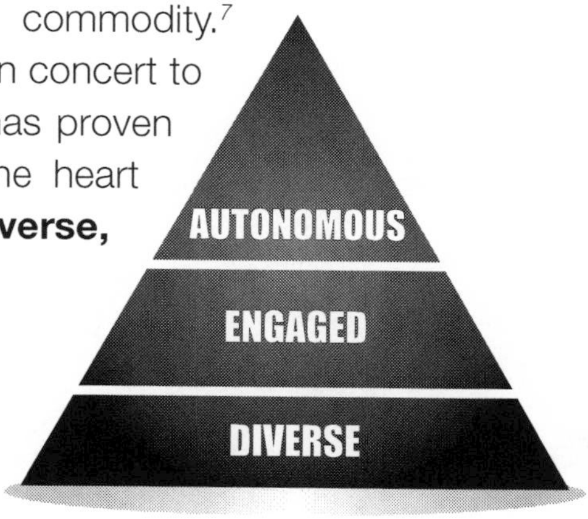

Figure 9 The People Triangle

DIVERSE

Mention the word diversity in a workplace, and the reaction you often get is, "Yeah, we know it…equality and inclusion." Most people have a narrow view of the word diversity. The real case for diversification is that teams get exponentially better at solving tougher problems when they incorporate diverse perspectives, backgrounds, and talents.

While individuals will always come up with novel ideas, when it comes to developing and monetizing ideas, study after study reveal a few key things. Teams produce innovation, especially when they're cognitively diverse. Teams of four to eight are better functioning than larger or smaller sizes. Teams need to collaborate, communicate, and confront (argue) to be effective.

AUTONOMOUS

ENGAGED

DIVERSE

Cognitive Diversity—Research

Cognitive diversity, according to the University of Michigan professor Scott Page, is "…how people see, categorize, understand and go about improving the world." Cognitive diversity is comprised of several key elements:

- **Diverse Perspectives**—people "see" and envision the world and its possibilities differently. A foodie will see a French restaurant much differently than a Weight Watcher!

- **Diverse Interpretations** is about how we categorize the world. If you give a random group of words to doctors and lawyers, they will sort them quite differently—especially if the keyword is malpractice!

- **Diverse Heuristics** give us rules of thumb to generate solutions. So, rules like, when someone's bleeding, stop the bleeding. Or, drink more water in the summer to stay healthy.

- **Diverse Predictive Models** give us approaches to infer cause. If-then statements help people solve problems.

When looking at complex problems, combining these four elements leads toward powerful solutions to difficult issues.[8] In his definitive book, *The Difference: How the Power of Diversity Creates Better Groups, Firms, Schools, and Societies,* Professor Scott Page asserts that cognitive diversity is not about identity diversity (male v. family, black v. white or old v. young), although identity and cognitive diversity complement each other well. In fact, real progress on problem-solving "...depends as much on our collective differences as it does on our individual IQ scores."[9] Indeed, diversity trumps ability. With disjunctive tasks like solving a complex math problem, when one person solves it, the entire group benefits. Diversity works well with such disjunctive tasks wherein several people try to solve the task or problem but where one good approach can help all. In teams, such divergent thinking is critical and helps avoid a more dangerous outcome: Groupthink—converging on a single solution too quickly and ignoring other, different possibilities. Here's what *Psychology Today* has to say about the dangers of groupthink:

Groupthink occurs when a group of well-intentioned people make irrational or non-optimal decisions that are spurred by the urge to conform or the discouragement of dissent. This problematic or premature consensus may be fueled by an agenda or simply because group members value harmony and coherence above rational thinking. In a groupthink situation, group members refrain from expressing doubts and judgments or disagreeing with the consensus. In the interest of making a decision that furthers their group's cause, members may ignore any ethical or moral consequences. Risky or disastrous military maneuvers, such as the escalation of the Vietnam War or the invasion of Iraq are commonly cited as instances of groupthink. The term was first introduced in the November 1971 issue of *Psychology Today*, in an article by psychologist Irving Janis, who had conducted extensive study of group decision-making under conditions of stress.[10]

Groupthink is how indefensible wars start. Groupthink is how people get convicted of crimes they did not commit. Groupthink is how groups can make terrible decisions—especially under a confident, albeit misinformed, leader who punishes people for disagreement.

On the other hand, distributed problem solving creates a situation where many people using different tools can look differently at the same problem. This increases the chances of finding a better solution faster. Thus, open-source projects with many diverse contributors, who provide a kind of checks-and-balances on discovering the truth—like Wikipedia and Threadless—lead to innovation. Finally, culture (norms and modes of behavior) must include collaboration, communication, and confrontation for decentralized organizational problem solving and innovation to take hold in organizations. Apple's Steve Jobs summed this up with two words, "Think Different," which, despite the grammatical gaffe, gets to the heart of innovation and adaptation.[11]

Cognitive Diversity—Personality Types

Let's say you've been asked to lead a new team. It doesn't much matter what kind of team. How would you begin to apply all the research about cognitive diversity? Of course, one way would be to recruit people from very diverse backgrounds— not only gender or race but also education, experience, social difference, and so on. You want people who come from multi-varied perspectives to look at the same problem with differing sets of eyes.

If you have the time and ability to recruit that kind of diversity, great. But what about when you inherit an intact team and must work with the team you've been given? Sure, over time, you could onboard diverse new team members. But that might take years. So, besides hiring consultants to make up the difference you need, what else can you do?

We suggest that you figure out what strengths and abilities you already have on the current team. One easy way to approach cognitive diversity is by way of personality types. There are many assessment instruments out there that assess aspects of personality: StrengthsFinder®, the VIA Survey, the Myers-Briggs Type Indicator (MBTI®), the Big 5, DISC®, and others. When a team takes the same instrument and simply shares the results, a new level of understanding emerges. Suddenly, people learn that not everyone thinks the same way they do—an obvious but huge revelation for teams. When this happens, teams become more effective and efficient simply by knowing where certain strengths on a team might be found.

Moreover, new research by Anita Wooley at Carnegie Mellon tells us that knowing which specific assignments to task to specific people makes sense, but now we have the data to prove it.[12] Her work also indicates that effective teams function like a whole brain. Connected, integrated, and varying personality types working in concert have the same effect.

The Jungian personality model focuses on four pairs of polar opposites: Extraversion vs. Introversion—where people get energy from; Sensing vs. Intuition—how they get information; Thinking vs. Feeling—how they think and make decisions based on the information; and finally, Judging vs. Perceiving—how they relate to the world.

For the purposes of this discussion, we'll consider a combination of the middle two elements of the Jungian assessment, which are known as the cognitive elements (how we think and decide): ST, SF, NF, NT.

- STs are tactical thinkers. They are good with data and detail—the more the better. They tend to be linear, logical, and literal. "What you see is what you get" might be their philosophy. They make great data gatherers, analysts, and organizers of people and things. They often find their way into engineering, analytics, and computer science—data-based professions. STs often end up leading teams and organizations.

- SFs are tactical feelers. They are not only good with data and detail, but also working with people. So, while they possess the same data-based characteristics as STs, they're more prone to exercise people-oriented, pro-social behavior and less logical rigor in their decision making. They are the social glue that keeps teams together. They often end up in service-oriented careers—healthcare, teaching, and ministry.

- NFs are strategic feelers and big-picture oriented— more about creativity and innovation and less about history and facts. They're also excellent working with people. These are the people with the big ideas who can also sell the ideas throughout the organization. They often end up in jobs like teachers, salespeople, and presenters.

- NTs are strategic thinkers and big picture folks—more strategic and less tactical than STs and SFs. NTs have a certain intellectual rigor about them. Interested in big ideas, NTs will attack problems using a rigorous logical progression. NTs often end up leading teams and organizations. They become doctors, lawyers, and college professors.

When teams form, it's a great idea to have them all take the Jungian assessment and then just extract the two cognitive elements. This enables the team members to understand each other as they begin a task so they can work together more effectively. Consider the matrix team operating model employed by some consulting companies. Teams form, solve problems or meet needs, disband and reform with different people on the team. Getting to know each other quickly is critically important when the team doesn't have years to connect and gel. Regardless of the personality instrument companies might use to help people understand differences, using an assessment tool early in the team-forming process offers team members valuable insights into personality that can build and not detract from team effectiveness.

Cognitive Diversity—Team Size

In the case of teams, size matters. In the military, typically a squad is composed of two or three rifle teams of four soldiers each. One of the original reasons was that in the heat of battle, you could only hear the orders if you were in a small deployment of troops. Research about complex problem solving—action learning—by Reg Ravens at the University of Cambridge's world-famous Cavendish Laboratory discovered that a group of four to eight people was the ideal team size needed to solve such big problems effectively.[13] Any less than that and you'll lose the power of diverse thinking. Any more and it's hard to coordinate the team effectively. Today, major organizations around the world use Raven's system and team-size recommendations. Famed Harvard professor Richard Hackman, who has studied teams for many years, said that any team larger than nine becomes ineffective.

One key reason is based on network theory. According to Robert Metcalfe's research, Metcalfe's law states the effect of a communications network is proportional to the square of the number of connected users of the system.[14] Say what? This just means that the more people you add to a group, the more geometrically complex that system becomes and the more difficult it is to maintain close relationships.

For example:

2 team members	=	1 connection
3 team members	=	3 connections
4 team members	=	6 connections
6 team members	=	15 connections
16 team members	=	120 connections

One interesting application of group size takes place at universities, specifically within MBA programs, which use small learning teams to enhance the depth of education. What size? Five to six people. Note that at the University of Virginia's Darden MBA program, a lot of thought goes into just who those people are— such as age, gender, race, experience, and more.[15] Darden's focus: Get as diverse a group as possible so they can work together to solve problems and learn.

ENGAGED

Just as organizations are larger gatherings of teams, teams are smaller gatherings of people. As we look at teams, we'll first explore the fundamentals of what makes people tick and, then, see what leaders can do to make them tick together in synchrony.

We've all seen people who love the work they do. They have an infectious energy, zest, and enthusiasm about them. Conversely, we've watched people at work who seem lifeless, as if their souls have been sucked out of them by their work.

So, what's the secret?

People with enthusiasm and zest have learned how to engage both their cognitive strengths and character strengths at work and on the team. For teams and organizations to be successful, you need people working in their strengths and to be fully engaged. The first step is to identify their strengths using reliable tools.

Cognitive Strengths

In the previous section, we described the Jungian model of personality, specifically cognitive strengths—how people think differently and, thus, how they approach solving problems with differing strengths. As we discussed, a tactical thinker (ST) would take a much more analytical approach to a problem than, for example, a strategic feeler (NF). If they were both writers, the tactical thinker (ST) would be disposed to writing nonfiction books based on data and facts. However, if STs venture into fiction, it often looks more like a Tom Clancy novel, full of specific details, whereas the strategic feeler (NF), would be more like Stephen King—a more creative, fanciful writer.

So now, after describing cognitive differences, we'll look at character strengths as a second aspect to consider when pulling together engaged teams.

Character Strengths

Personal values are at the very heart of what motivates us and who we are—our basic character. Motivation is at the heart of engagement. People engage when what they're doing relates to what they value. Such motivation is intrinsic and imbedded into our values system. Studies by Gallup show that engagement accounts for a 30% difference in productivity. On the negative end, disengagement creates toxic workers who greatly damage the team and organization. Finally, negative, disengaged people pull down the team's performance.

Positive psychologists Martin Seligman and Chris Peterson sought to find an alternative approach to psychology and mental health—different from the traditional disorder-approach (the what's-wrong-with-me approach), which is based on the Diagnostic and Statistical Manual of Mental Disorders (DSM).

So, they developed the Character Strengths and Virtues Handbook (CSV), which classifies positive character strengths. Funded by a grant from the Mayerson Foundation, Seligman and Peterson engaged many of the leading social scientists of our day and scoured the science, cultures, and religions for a common, accepted set of universal values. Thus, the writings of Aristotle, Plato, Confucius, Lao Tzu, and many others were studied. Religions like Buddhism, Islam, Taoism, Judaism, and Catholicism were also studied for common sets of values and virtues. The research of renowned psychologists and scholars like Maslow, Erickson, Thorndike, and Gardner was studied as well.

The cumulative result of this prodigious effort across cultures and time was the identification of 24 character strengths that fell within six critical, universal categories or virtues that combine to help people (especially teams) become more diverse, balanced, and effective. What follows is a description of those critical six categories of virtues and the character strengths associated with each in the values in action (VIA) classification.[16]

- **Wisdom:** Comes from the bumps and scrapes of life—learning gained from experience that can be applied in the future for good. It's not IQ, but a kind of street smarts, or as authors call it, "noble intelligence." *The character strengths associated with wisdom are creativity, curiosity, judgment (critical thinking), love of learning, and perspective.*

- **Courage:** Overcoming fear—physical or psychological. Facing our fears doesn't demand a grand heroic act or effort. Rather, it's about facing the daily moments of bravery at home and at work. *The character strengths associated with courage are bravery, perseverance, honesty, and zest.*

- **Humanity:** Altruistic acts of service to others, positive social behavior, and generosity of spirit are the hallmarks of this virtue. *The character strengths associated with humanity are love, kindness, and social intelligence.*

- **Justice:** Fairness and equity regarding the level of our contribution and reward mark this virtue. "Giving and getting your fair share" would be the motto of this virtue in action. *The character strengths associated with justice are fairness, leadership, and teamwork.*

- **Temperance:** Control, moderation, and self-restraint mark this virtue. Temperance shows up in people as being in control of their emotions and behaviors, not given to excess, and as self-denial in service to others. *The character strengths associated with temperance are forgiveness (mercy), humility (modesty), prudence, and self-regulation.*

- **Transcendence:** People who crave meaning and purpose in their lives possess this virtue. They seek connection to beliefs and goals bigger than themselves. *The character strengths associated with temperance are appreciation of beauty and excellence, gratitude, hope, humor, and spirituality.*

The VIA character strengths instrument surfaces what intrinsically motivates us—a critically important finding. Character strengths are the key to how leaders can specifically motivate individuals. Match tasks to character strengths and watch people light up, going from "must do" to "want to do" more. Character strengths are positive strengths focused on thinking and behaving in ways that benefit yourself and others.

Character strengths are different from cognitive strengths—what we are naturally good at, like influencing, strategic thinking, or building relationships. Character strengths amplify, even turbocharge, those cognitive strengths and provide the best path to them. So, a strategic feeler (NF) with high scores in the virtue category of wisdom—like character strengths of love of learning and creativity—will enjoy a highly creative writing assignment that requires learning and a varied work environment over a routine one. A tactical thinker (ST) with high scores in the virtue of courage—like character strengths of honesty and bravery—might like to tackle a more complex, difficult organizational problem that requires confronting the brutal facts of the situation.

Research indicates that engaging our VIA character strengths reduces stress and dysfunction and amplifies positivity. Specific impacts of values engagement are found in the following: Greater happiness, acceptance of oneself, reverence for life, competence, mental and physical health, positive and supportive social networks, engaging and meaningful work, accomplishment of goals, greater engagement and life meaning, higher work productivity, increased likelihood of work being a life calling, less stress and improved coping, greater academic achievement, improved close relationships.[17]

Generally, character strengths are closely associated with positive psychology and well-being. When people are working with their character strengths, like using a favorite tool, they build better things like relationships, businesses, products, and services. Harvard professor Howard Gardner, one of the country's most respected scholars, said the following about character research. *"Peterson and Seligman's endeavor to focus on human strengths and virtues is one of the most important initiatives in psychology of the past half century."*[18]

How do character strengths interact with work tasks? When we use character strengths, like hope and humility, while facing the task of crafting a corporate strategy, we're more disposed to face the future with more positive energy and engagement. Or, when you're asked to teach a compliance class that everyone hates, but you deliver it with zest and honesty, the whole thing becomes more fun both for the class and the instructor. The reason: You're tapping into intrinsic values, which are the highest motivators. They don't just keep you involved but fully engage you. When that engagement is sustained over time, it produces people with more of a "calling" attitude toward their work and less of a job-like attitude. Imagine the opposite, using tools you don't like at work every day without a break. Soon, you're into a 9-5 situation, staring at the clock, and counting the minutes until you can leave.

Reinforcing the importance of engagement, two professors at the Stanford Design School—Bill Burnett and Dave Evans—have told us just how to build a better, more engaged life in their book, *Designing Your Life: How to Build a Well-Lived, Joyful Life.* They explain that most of us don't know what we're going to do in life. Only 27% of college grads get to practice their majors on the job. In the U.S., over 66% of people dislike their work, and 15% hate it! Success doesn't make you happy. Finding work that fits you makes you happy. In the U.S., 31 million people (ages 44-70) want a career with meaning, income, and purpose. Unfortunately, we try to find our life's work by thinking ourselves toward it, when really "building" our way forward is most often how it really happens. A well-designed life is one that constantly adapts and stays open to wonder and surprise. The five steps of the Stanford Design process are curiosity (questions), trying stuff (a bias for action), reframing problems, knowing it's a process, and asking others for help.[19]

How Leaders Can Use
Character and Cognitive Strengths

Our hypothesis is that people can find their highest and best use in society by simply employing both of these assessments. It's a bit like knowing that a clean diet, exercise, and sleep are all important for your health. People who engage in all three are likely to be the healthiest in their age group.

Continuing research indicates that character strengths may act as a kind of supercharger of our cognitive strengths. To best direct people's work or even their careers, here's an exercise a leader might use:

- Ask team members to take the VIA Character Strengths assessment. The results will highlight their top character strengths across the six major categories—the Virtues (Wisdom, Courage, Humanity, Justice, Temperance, and Transcendence). See virtues and character strengths mentioned in the above section. Then, determine Virtues (in Character Strengths) where the person has two or more strengths. Also, pay special attention to the #1 or #2 character strengths. Note: This instrument is free at www.viacharacter.org.

- Next, ask each team member to take the free Jungian online assessment at www.123test.com. Then ask them to determine their cognitive type. The instrument will yield four-letter designations, such as ISTJ (tactical thinker) or ENFJ (strategic feeler). The two middle letters act as the cognitive types—above see ST and NF highlighted.

- Finally, pull character strengths together with cognitive strengths and use them both as filters when looking at potential future work.

- Case Example: Mary is a tactical feeler (SF). She has two character-based strengths—kindness and social intelligence—in the category of Humanity in the VIA Character Survey.

  - So, giving her a job that routinely requires her to punish people for lack of policy compliance or having to lay off people would ultimately drive her away from the company if she was forced to do that for a prolonged period.

  - However, matching her with a position that helps people come together and work as a team would be right up her alley. Her social intelligence would become the very glue that binds the team. She would be totally engaged and cement her job satisfaction and engagement beyond anything a leader could say or do to motivate her. In fact, this kind of thoughtful assignment separates successful and mediocre leaders and companies.

- **Align Your Strengths to Your Role on the Team.** Now, it's your turn. Try taking some assessments like the ones described above to understand your character strengths and your cognitive type. Review and think about how you could use this information to have a greater impact on the team. Share your thoughts with your team leader and see if there is an opportunity to align your work better with your strengths.

AUTONOMOUS

If you've ever worked for a micromanaging boss or been assigned to an over-directed team led by a suffocating, domineering leader, you will like what comes next.

Research confirms that people and teams want autonomy to make their own decisions. Period!

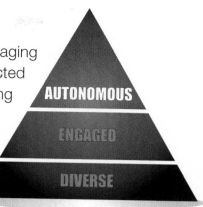

Abraham Maslow showed us this in his hierarchy of needs,[20] and Frederick Herzberg demonstrated the power of autonomy and purpose in his workplace-setting experiments when he developed his two-factor theory.[21] Numerous other psychologists have emphasized the basic need for autonomy. More recently, in his book *Drive!*, bestselling author Dan Pink talks about autonomy as one of several fundamental motivators: autonomy, mastery and purpose. So, let's start with the individual and then discuss teams.

Autonomous people

For years, the predominant leadership model has been command and control: Do it because I say so or because I'm in charge and know better. The controlling model still works in the military, law enforcement, and with first responders where immediacy saves lives. However, even for those emergency workers, such as police officers, it's used less than 10% of the time.[22]

In the past, an emerging, autonomous model has worked informally, but today it's being used more purposefully. It's called the Coach-Approach model,[23] where leaders ask questions rather than give answers. With this autonomous approach, it's the followers, not the leader, who are in control. While this may be somewhat awkward for some to adopt at first, once it's used regularly with practice, people begin to see results—autonomy, trust, confidence, and better relationships with the leader. This model consists of four steps: Problem, Present, Possible, and Plan—the 4-P's.

Coach-Approach Model

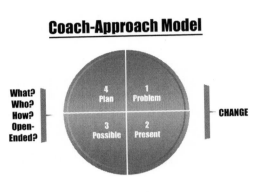

This model works well with either individual people or with teams. With individuals, first the leader-coach asks questions to identify the problem: What seems to be the biggest issue you're facing? What does it look like? Second, the leader-coach tries to establish the extent of the problem, the present state, with several questions, such as: On a scale from 1-10 (low to high), how much is this problem impacting you or others? Third, the leader-coach asks questions around what the possible future could look like: What is your ideal vision for the future regarding this issue/problem? What would it look like if it was solved? Finally, the leader-coach seeks action and accountability around the plan forward: What's one step you might take to solve this problem? What will you need? When will you get it done?

For a deeper explanation of the Coach-Approach model, check out our book, *Leading Well,* on Amazon.

Autonomous teams

While individuals benefit and gain autonomy from coaching, groups and teams reap even more strategic benefits because of their collective impact on the organization and even on each other in the process. While we described this difference previously, it's worth reconsidering.

At work, the group-vs-team distinction is present. Consider a sales team, with reps in multiple locations in charge of their own territories. While the revenue gets collected and counted as a team, most often the reps act like independent owners. On the other hand, IT teams are far more interdependent. What the systems engineer does is affected by how the systems architect designs the system, and so on. Groups are more independent but related. Teams are interdependent and rely very much on each other.

Both teams and groups require coordination. The larger the gathering, the more coordination required. You need a traffic cop of sorts to direct, but not drive, the traffic. Thus, the big difference between one-on-one coaching and team coaching is that with a team or group, a coach facilitates the process. This requires questions and the coaching process to evolve.

The roots for good team or group coaching lie in a process called "action learning," originally developed in England by Reg Revans and refined over the years. As a doctoral student at the world-renowned Cavendish Labs at Cambridge University in England—home to an astonishing twenty-nine Nobel Prize winners—Revans captured their largely inquisitive discovery process, codified it, and developed a replicable process for companies.[24] His work has been refined and developed in the United States by scholars such as Michael Marquardt at The George Washington University. Marquadt taught the process widely and founded the World Institute for Action Learning[25] to spread the word. With some simple rules and discipline, this process can be adapted quickly to most meetings.

The basic several-to-one team-coaching requirements

- **Coach:** You need someone to act as the coach in charge of the process but not participate directly in the problem solving. This can be the team leader, an external coach, or even someone on the team who steps out of the problem solving and plays this role.

- **Participants:** Four to eight people works best. If you have fewer than four people, you'll lose the power of cognitive diversity—people thinking differently about the same problem. With more than eight people, you'll have trouble just getting the meeting to happen and keeping it controlled and effective.

- **Rules:**

    - The coach can stop and start the dialogue at any time.

    - Participants are only allowed to ask questions. Statements are allowed only if responding to a direct question.

    - Anyone can ask a question to anyone else in the group.

- **Questions:** Should be information-seeking. Open-ended questions like Who, What, How, When, and even Why are best. Yes-or-No questions do not work well as they shut the dialogue down.

- **Process:** Using the Coach-Approach process works well—Problem, Present, Possible, and Plan.

If you've ever sat through an endless, painful, and rambling committee or staff meeting, this coaching technique will make you want to jump with joy. The critical problem with most group meetings, regardless of size, is a woeful lack of both a structure and an approach focused on mindful reflection. What follows are two ways to use coaching, both for team coaching (several-to-one coaching) and large-group coaching (one-to-many coaching).

TEAM COACHING

Just as one-on-one coaching provides an opportunity to reflect and thoughtfully solve problems, team coaching amplifies the experience. Four to five people coaching one person happens best when one of the participants acts as the managing coach. The managing coach ensures that the other participants follow the Coach-Approach process—asking questions, not giving advice. Sounds easy, but when you increase the number of participants in the coaching process, the job of the managing coach becomes critical to success. It's like the difference between having one child or having three. One child is a big wave in the ocean of your life, but three is like a tsunami!

The protocol starts with the coach reminding everyone in the group about the three simple, but powerful, rules of coaching. Next, the coach draws the basic Coach-Approach model on the board as a roadmap for decision making.

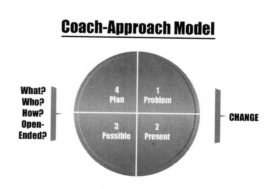

Coach-Approach Model

Then, the managing coach (or professional coach if one is brought in) opens by asking the problem owner to give a brief (5 minutes or less) overview of the problem s/he faces.

Following that, the coach asks who has the first question about the problem. Then, the coach monitors the group—insuring that people stick to curiosity, ask open-ended questions, and refrain from giving answers or advice. A key role the coach must play is keeping the group from acting like consultants and offering solutions before the group figures out what the real problem is. It's worth noting that most problems or issues raised rarely turn out to be the real problem, rather the symptom of the dysfunction that gets uncovered by good coaching.

The managing coach will take the team through the same steps as in one-on-one coaching: problem, present, possible, and plan. After each of the questions are asked by team members and there appears to be a clear starting point reached in the plan moving forward, the coach will ask what the team will do first, when it will get done, and how the group will know it's been done. Thus, there is strict accountability for action. Coaching is about making intentional change.

One-to-Many Coaching

As in team coaching, one person must fill the role of coach to ensure the group focuses on the Coach-Approach process—asking questions, not giving advice. With a much larger crowd in the room, the coach acts like a traffic cop at the center of a busy intersection—keeping cars flowing by stopping some and waving on others—per a proven process.

To get an idea about how this works, picture 25 people in a room. The coach steps to the front of the conference room like a facilitator and draws the Coach-Approach model on the

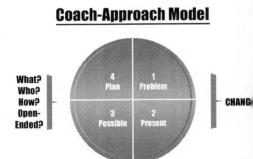

Coach-Approach Model

What? Who? How? Open-Ended?

4 Plan	1 Problem
3 Possible	2 Present

CHANG

board. This will act as the group's roadmap for the session. Next, the coach will state, in general terms, what the meeting is about. Let's say it's to expand the company's market. The coach announces this and asks people to write a sentence or two about what they individually think the real problem is. Next, the coach puts them in groups of four to six people and asks each group to work on developing a group definition of the problem. When they are done, the coach asks each group to report out and capture the feedback offered by each group, preferably on a flip chart or whiteboard at the front of the room. Some discussion ensues and the coach asks people to rank the definitions from the groups based on which one they believe aligns closest to the actual issue. Eventually, the coach gets them to agree on the best definition of the problem to work on.

This kind of coaching facilitation takes place with every question focused on the model (Problem, Present, Possible, Plan). For example, next, the coach will ask all the groups to make a list of the current impact the selected problem is having on the company. The groups discuss and come up with a list and the coach gathers, refines, and ranks their findings. By the end of the discussion, the coach will have led the groups to define the ideal future state. Subsequently, they will develop a plan—a list of next steps to accomplish and who will be responsible for each action. Thus, an often rambling, even unruly group gets offered a disciplined way to start to solve a complex problem with collective brainpower.

Hopefully, by now, you see the need for diverse, engaged, and autonomous people and teams. But people can't do it alone—they need a leader. In the next chapter, we'll discuss the critical elements for great leadership centered around the most fundamental element between people: **trust.**

03: LEADER

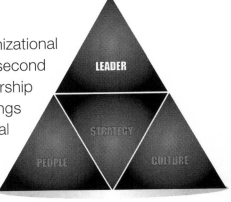

Figure 10 *The Team Leadership Pyramid: Leader*

Every significant team and organizational effort start with a leader—the second critical element in the Team Leadership Pyramid. Without a leader, things don't happen. Whether it's a social situation, like planning a trip or a gathering, or agreeing to head up a working group in an organization, someone must step up and say, "I'll do it." Without a leader, ideas falter because groups don't naturally galvanize and engage as teams—they stand around until a leader emerges.

It's why we have athletic coaches, principals of schools, CEOs, and political leaders. In earlier days, we had chiefs and tribal leaders. For example, amidst chaos in failed, lawless countries, tribal leaders or overlords of factions evolved. It's basic survival instinct at work. Even in the animal kingdom, the phenomenon exists in a more primal way—packs of wolves, hyenas, and prides of lions. All creatures seek a leader to keep them safe, connected, and focused on things that matter.

Trust is at the very core of leadership.

Here's some current research about the central importance of trust from *The Mind of a Leader,* published by the Harvard Business Press.

...CEOs recognize that trust is an issue foremost in the minds of their employees. The 2016 PwC global CEO survey reported that 55 percent of CEOs think that a lack of trust is a threat to their organizational growth. In 2014, just two years earlier, this number was 37 percent. Hold this number against the results of the Edelman Trust Barometer global annual survey of 2017, which found that 63 percent of employees said that CEOs are "not at all, or somewhat credible." Similarly, Ernst & Young's Trust in the Workplace found that only 46 percent of employees place trust in their employer. Trust matters in business and in leadership.[26]

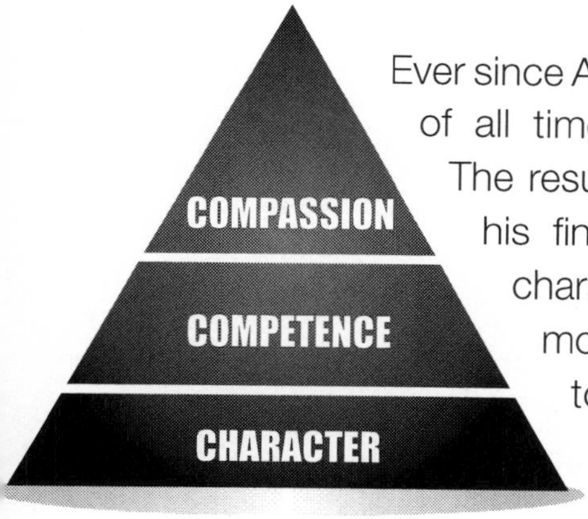

Figure 11 The Trust Triangle

Ever since Aristotle, one of the greatest thinkers of all time, our society has studied trust. The results have remained consistent with his findings—we seek people of good character, good deeds, and good will. In modern terms, the model boils down to three essential elements (The 3-Cs): **character, competence,** and **compassion**. In an earlier book, *The Trusted Leader,* we called this The Trust Triangle. While we ended up using Aristotle's language in the book, when we teach the concepts these days, the 3-Cs seem more relevant and easier for people to both understand and remember.

CHARACTER

Trusted leaders are honest and dependable.

Their character demonstrates candor, communication skill, and courage. Character forms the fundamental basis of trust—thus it is at the very base of the trust triangle. Let's look at several key elements of character.

Candor. *Trusted leaders are honest, sincere, and forthright with themselves and others.*

Candor with others—other awareness—mirrors the need for self-awareness. It's also a key element of emotional intelligence. You might say that other awareness is the opposite side of the self-awareness coin. Living up to our word, living into the values we espouse, and doing what we say we will do, all frame the contours of other awareness. We all want to live and work with people who do what they say they will do, who tell the truth, and are reliable. At the heart of all that is candor. When developing his Beliefs, Attitude, and Values theory, social scientist Milton Rokeach studied the values that Americans hold near and dear to their hearts.[27] In survey after survey, the undisputed #1 pick was honesty—candor. Leaders who are honest, authentic (self-aware), and other-aware develop better teams and organizations. In fact, within the FBI, candor still remains one of the central standards. Doing something wrong—depending on the severity of it—is not usually the biggest problem, but lying about it is.

Communication. *Trusted leaders speak, write, and listen well.*

Speaking: Leaders who can articulate their vision will move followers toward their goals faster and more surely. Speaking well starts with interpersonal communication—sitting down and talking to another person. While fundamental, this is sometimes difficult. Focusing on the other person—offering eye contact, facing each other, gesturing, encouraging, and above all listening—form the most basic of interpersonal skills. In fact, listening is the flip side of speaking. While speaking well to people, teams, groups, and boards is also critical, if you must pick one skill to develop, practice listening, and see how people begin to consider you a great conversationalist! If people leave a conversation with you where they feel like they talked most of the time, they'll think it was a great conversation.

Writing: Being able to write will always be a fundamental skill for leaders. Whether it's a text, email, or a report, clear and concise writing gets rewarded with attention and influence. Also, understanding the writing style and personality preferences of our key audiences has been found to be critical. Personality influences our writing styles and, effectively, our success in organizations.[28] In *WriteType: Personality Types and Writing Styles,* we explain just how this dynamic works in detail.

Listening: Of all the skills great leaders demonstrate, listening is #1. Why? The very act of listening raises the status of the other person in the conversation.[29] Such attention shows that leaders care about what the other person thinks, thus bestowing increased status on him/her. Statistically, we know that leaders prefer to talk rather than listen even though leaders who listen are rated significantly higher.[30] When leaders fall in love with their own voices, people tune out the rhetoric. An article from the Harvard Business Review recommends a form of 360-degree listening.[31] Listen to what the other person is saying, how they're saying it, and what they're not saying. People tell the truth very generally but lie very specifically.

Courage. *Trusted Leaders speak truth to power.*

When we hear the word "courage," most people envision a police officer running to help someone in distress, a fireman rushing into a burning building, or a soldier heroically saving a wounded buddy in combat. While those are certainly dramatic examples of courage, it's the day-to-day courage that's most enduring and often the most difficult to face up to. For example, when you're in a meeting and everyone is voting to take a strategic path, but you have data that supports a different path, many people are disposed to go along with the group—this is called the bandwagon effect—and not upsetting the status quo. However, it takes a real leader to step up and tell the truth amidst pressure to conform.

If you want to see this kind of leadership courage in action, watch the classic movie *12 Angry Men,* starring Henry Fonda. He methodically refutes each juror empaneled on a murder case. A more recent example was an organization's board that was tasked to consider moving out the CEO. When it came to a Yea-or-Nay vote, several voted not to fire him and to give him yet another chance. The voting was deadlocked. Then, a female executive stood up and courageously challenged them all to rethink what they were doing and how they'd treat this CEO if he was an employee. She stood up for what she believed in, and eventually, all in the meeting knew that they needed to remove this CEO for the good of the organization and, frankly, for himself. They did so in a revote—thanks to her courage.

COMPETENCE

Trusted Leaders possess, seek, and share knowledge.

Competence is the next level of the trust triangle. It's about both a personal and professional capacity—knowing what they are doing. Great leaders have self-awareness, understand and respect differences in others and know their profession— lawyers and doctors lead law firms and medical practices.

Self-Awareness: *Trusted leaders know who they are.*

Several times a month, we have conversations with executives who want to refer others in their companies to coaching, without really understanding how coaching works. The conversation always has a big "but" in the middle of it. "Joe is a great guy, smart as heck—went to MIT for his engineering degree and Harvard for his MBA— *but* nobody trusts him!" The most common reason for the big "but" is that, often, the person being referred to has poor self-awareness. In fact, self-awareness comprises one of the baseline elements of emotional intelligence.[32] The gap between what we consider our strengths and challenges and what others think they are is what might be termed as our "self-awareness" deficit. The larger that gap, the more serious the problem for leaders. While we all have blind spots, a large gap in self-awareness leads to mistrust, misfires, and mishaps. One of our executive clients once thought she was a strong, decisive leader who made good decisions and solved problems. However, the people who worked for her thought of her as a self-centered narcissist, incapable of thinking or caring about others. Despite all attempts to help her modify her behavior, she refused to budge and was eventually forced out. Candor means first and foremost being honest, starting with yourself—self-awareness. When leaders are in touch with who they are, warts and all, they—and the people they lead—enjoy a more fruitful, positive, and productive relationship.

Other Awareness: *Trusted leaders learn about, understand, and respect differences in others.*

The saying "different horses for different courses" helps explain the importance of knowing others. You wouldn't think of taking the winner of the Kentucky Derby and hitching that horse to a plow. Yet, we try to force people of all kinds to conform to one-size-fits-all job descriptions. Then, when people fail, we wonder what went wrong or search for personality defects to "fix." Everyone has a set of core talents—things they're naturally good at. Gallup has been at the center of focusing us on 34 talents, which when practiced, lead to individual strengths. Playing to people's strengths makes a huge difference in both personal and team performance. Trying to only fix weaknesses instead of working on strengths can be a colossal waste of time. Leaders who play to people's strengths excel.

Know What They're Doing: *Trusted leaders have a level of competence in their professions that earns the respect of followers.*

Imagine a chief of police who never spent much time on the street as a patrol officer. Imagine the chief of medicine in a hospital who was never a practicing physician, or the managing partner of a law firm who had a law degree but never practiced law. We want leaders who know what they're doing and have been "in the trenches." But also note that it's often not the smartest doctor or lawyer or the highest ranking salesperson who makes the best leader. For example, when companies promote the best salesperson to sales manager, they often lose a great sales producer and gain a bad manager—what I call a leadership double whammy.

Trusted leaders continuously learn and adapt to the world. Becoming a lifelong learner has been the mantra of the Association for Talent Development (ATD) because research supports the many benefits of continued curiosity.[33] There's a reason that nearly every profession requires continuing education courses to remain certified, from medicine to law and from psychology to coaching. Unfortunately, at this time there is no requirement for continuing education for many organizational leadership roles, but perhaps that will change in the future.

Trusted leaders share what they know with others. Working with our leadership clients, we tell them upfront that their main job is to produce future leaders—in a sense, train their replacements. Secure leaders understand intuitively that all of life is succession planning. We have children—the ultimate succession plan! No children and society evaporates. No future leaders and companies evaporate. Therefore, trusted leaders create a learning environment. They send people to be trained, create in-house training and development programs, and grow strong mentoring programs at every level of the organization.

COMPASSION

Trusted leaders are compassionate— they step up to help others in need.

In *The Mind of the Leader: How to Lead Yourself, Your People and Your Organization for*

Extraordinary Results, a recent book published by the *Harvard Business Review*, numerous interviews of executives were conducted to understand highly successful leaders of today. The findings indicate that effective leaders have three things in common: mindfulness, they are present; selflessness, the mission and others come first; and, compassion, they care about and help others. According to the research, compassion is about having positive intentions for others and helping others in need. Empathy is absorbing the suffering of others, but compassion is taking action to relieve the suffering. Empathy is emotional and focuses on individuals, but compassion is rational and focuses on the greater good. Compassion fuels trust—fundamental to all relationships.[34]

Trusted leaders are compassionate with themselves—self-compassion. They're compassionate with others in the organization, not only feeling their emotion but reacting to it. They're also compassionate with others in the larger community around them.

Self-Compassion.

Trusted Leaders are kind to themselves, without being egocentric.

Compassion starts with yourself. It is an unconditional self-regard. Not in an egocentric, narcissistic way, but a pardoning of yourself with the same kindness you'd offer to a friend or family member. Thus, when you fail, simply say to yourself what you'd say to a friend who just failed. According to renowned compassion scholar, Kristen Neff, compassion consists of self-kindness, common humanity, and mindfulness. Self-kindness is about treating your shortcomings kindly and not engaging in self-criticism. Common humanity recognizes that failure and suffering are part of life. Mindfulness is a non-judgmental state of mind that allows us to look at our failures objectively.[35] Like everyone, leaders make mistakes. As a leader, if you're not making mistakes, you're likely too comfortable in your job and not growing. You have two options, to stay safe with the status quo, or stretch and grow. Self-compassion, like a good friend, will shore you up when you stub your toe.

Compassion for Others.

Trusted leaders care deeply and have strong relationships with others—social intelligence.

According to Daniel Goleman's well-respected research, emotional intelligence consists of self-awareness, self-regulation, motivation, empathy and social skills.[36] Basically, his theory focused on our emotional sense of self and others. Emotional self-awareness and other awareness give us distinct clues about how to interact with others. For example, when a leader's compassion is high on the emotional scale, respect and commitment come more easily. Thus, when a leader goes to the hospital to visit with an injured employee, it builds a bond of trust that can be extraordinary. Compassion for others is critical to team and organizational success. Trusted leaders notice, feel, and act on the pain and suffering of people in the organization.

The team and the organization become the environment where we live at work. It's quite literally our second home, and it can have a profound effect on our happiness and our health. Trusted leaders have a singular effect on the compassion within the organizational fabric—a kind of 'we care' attitude. Here's how the University of Michigan's Center for Positive Organizations describes it:

The authors of this article discuss the prevalence and costs of pain in organizational life and identify compassion as an important process that can occur in response to suffering. At the individual level, compassion takes place through three subprocesses: noticing another's pain, experiencing an emotional reaction to the pain, and acting in response to the pain. The authors build on this framework to argue that organizational compassion exists when members of a system collectively notice, feel, and respond to pain experienced by members of that system. These processes become collective as features of an organization's context, legitimize them within the organization, propagate them among organizational members, and coordinate them across individuals.[37]

Compassion for the Community, Country, and the World.

Trusted leaders focus out beyond themselves and even their organizations to the pain and suffering in their communities, country, and the world.

Just as we are nested in our work community, we are also citizens of our local, national, and, even more so, global neighborhood. What we do locally has consequences globally. It's no longer either good or smart to isolate ourselves. We're truly living in an interdependent world. We all want to not only live but also thrive. That's hard to do if our neighbors are polluting the same air and water we ingest—locally or globally. Author and speaker Karen Armstrong wanted to change that.[38]

A former Catholic nun, Armstrong now heads The Charter for Compassion, a powerful nonprofit that is focused on spreading compassion around the world. Her organization was funded by a $100,000 TED Talk grant. Much like the famed McArthur genius award, the TED Talk grant is given with no strings attached and is considered a major honor. Others who've received the award are Bill Clinton, E. O. Wilson, and others of that caliber. The Charter seeks to reduce suffering among humankind. It's based on the premise that every major religion on the earth supports the Golden Rule (Do unto others as you would have them do to you.). Any notion of putting a person, community, or country first is based on a faulty premise of threat and survival—stoked by humans' lower order brain—the ancient fight or flight response. Compassion, hope, and collaboration, not fight or flight, hold the promise of a thriving world at peace.

04: CULTURE

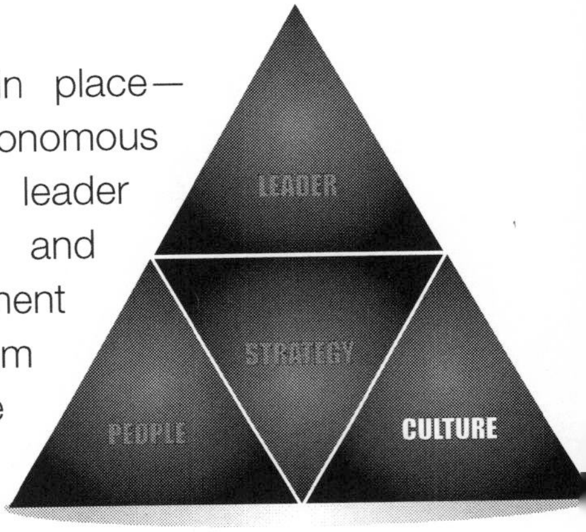

With two critical elements in place— diverse, engaged, and autonomous people, as well as a trusted leader with character, competence, and compassion—the next critical element of great teams is culture: the team environment. Culture is the invisible but powerful force, composed of symbols, values, beliefs, and assumptions nested within every team or organization that writes the

Figure 12 The Team Leadership Pyramid: Culture

"unwritten," but strictly enforced, rules. These invisible, but potent rules, maintain the status quo, by sending the message, "This is how we do things around here." If while reading this description of culture, you're thinking, "Hey, what about being an adaptive, innovative team?," just hold on a second.

Culture acts like the immune system for any team or organization from two to two thousand people. Thus, we can think about culture as a team, an organizational, even a national force. Culture protects the tribe from outsiders, who might corrupt or injure it. It acts very much like your own immune system: Identifies a foreign cell, such as a virus, and either allows it in after some powerful biological/cultural vetting; or, it rejects the virus outright. Therefore, when a new executive onboards into the organization and threatens the status quo too quickly by over-exerting authority, s/he gets what amounts to organ rejection from the team or organization. We've all seen a new leader come on board with all the promise in the world, only to be rejected in the first six months, never to fully recover from culture blowback.

There are ways to avoid such cultural rejection. When onboarding a new employee, especially an executive, we suggest going slow at first so you can go fast later.[39] We take up this same issue in the book, *Smile. Breathe. Listen: The 3 Mindful Acts for a Leader,* in which we suggest that just like medicine has its own oath, "First, do no harm," leadership should also have its own oath, "First, be no threat!"[40]

Further, at work, you have norms to protect your team, like when you refill the coffee, and where and when you work. It's no different in a domestic relationship. When people decide to live together, they begin to establish a culture and set up norms and rules of distributed work, appropriate behaviors, and standard procedures—who takes out the garbage, who cooks, who cleans, who locks up, who controls the thermostat, etc.

Like family culture, team culture is nested within other cultures depending on the size and scope of the company, such as the corporate, divisional, national, and regional cultures. For example, a company headquartered in Germany might be heavily influenced by the German culture, even to the regional offices in the Americas. Here's another way to look at the notion of nested cultures: Think about living in a country, state, city, or region. To illustrate this, let's say Joe lives in the United States where there is a culture of beliefs, such as freedom, independence, and opportunity. Joe lives in the state of Virginia, where there is a culture that includes the national cultural beliefs and then adds its own focus on education, government, and the military. Finally, Joe lives in Fairfax County. That adds even more cultural forces to the mix, such as technology, innovation, and higher education. People living in other, more rural areas of the state may have completely different regional customs and cultural rules.

The Culture Triangle

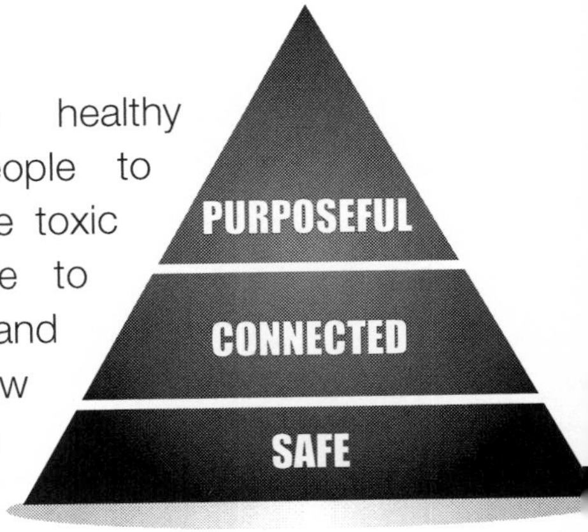

Some team cultures create healthy atmospheres and motivate people to thrive, but other cultures produce toxic atmospheres and cause people to disengage. Leaders must understand the critical elements that allow cultures to thrive. And because teams are where the action in the organization takes place, we place emphasis on team culture. Specifically, people need to feel **safe, connected, and purposeful**. We call this The Culture Triangle—a derivative from Maslow's Hierarchy of Needs.

Figure 13 The Culture Triangle

SAFE

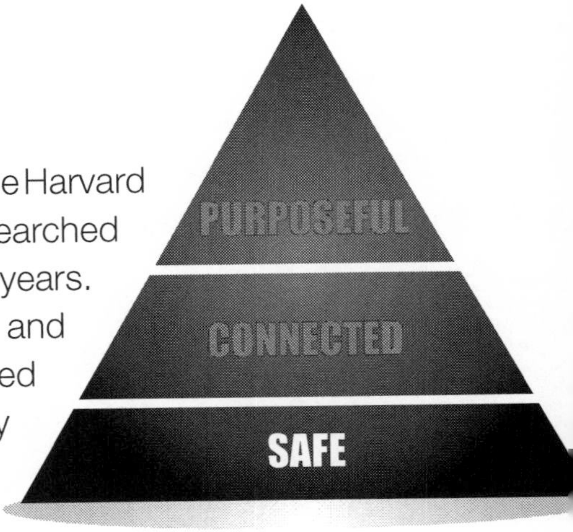

Professor Amy Edmondson at the Harvard Business School has researched successful teams for many years. She found that, in a complex and fast-moving economy, fixed teams as well as on-the-fly teaming is required to solve some of our toughest problems. In such ad hoc teams, we must gather people, focus them, and develop solutions to remain competitive as an organization. Command-

and-control leadership, which works in more predictable ways in manufacturing-based cultures, falls far short in knowledge-based and adaptive cultures. Teaming and collaboration that combine different talents, points of view, and perspectives capture value more readily in these more complex environments. The fundamentals of teaming, like taking risks, embracing failure, and crossing boundaries, feel unnatural to command-and-control cultures but are necessary if we are to compete successfully in today's world. Psychological safety is at the foundation of all great teams. Edmondson notes that "people fear being viewed as ignorant, incompetent, negative, or disruptive."[41] Thus, to be productive individually and as a team member, people must feel safe to say what they really think without any repercussions. Otherwise, they won't speak up, and the team and organization ultimately suffer.

Adding to Edmondson's research, Google has invested considerable time and money to research what makes a great leader (Project Oxygen) and what makes great teams (Project Aristotle). Project Oxygen identified the top 10 behaviors of Google's best managers/leaders.[42] Here they are listed in order of importance:

- Is a good coach

- Empowers the team and does not micromanage

- Creates an inclusive team environment, showing concern for success and well-being

- Is productive and results-oriented

- Is a good communicator — listens and shares information

- Supports career development and discusses performance

- Has a clear vision/strategy for the team

- Has key technical skills to help advise the team

- Collaborates across Google

- Is a strong decision-maker

In its related research referred to as Project Aristotle, Google studied 180 teams to conclude that, in the most effective teams, what really mattered was less about who was on the team, and more about how the team worked together. Here are their key team characteristics in order of importance:

- **Psychological Safety:** This concept refers to an individual's perception of the consequences of taking an interpersonal risk or a belief that a team is safe for risk-taking in the face of being considered ignorant, incompetent, negative, or disruptive. In a team with high psychological safety, teammates feel safe to take risks around their team members. They feel confident that no one on the team will embarrass or punish anyone else for admitting a mistake, asking a question, or offering a new idea.

- **Dependability:** On dependable teams, members reliably complete quality work on time versus the opposite—shirking responsibilities.

- **Structure and clarity:** An individual's understanding of job expectations, the process for fulfilling those expectations, and the consequences of one's performance are important for team effectiveness. Goals can be set at the individual or group level, and must be specific, challenging, and attainable. Google often uses Objectives and Key Results (OKRs) to help set and communicate short- and long-term goals.

- **Meaning:** Finding a sense of purpose in either the work itself or the output is important for team effectiveness. The meaning of the work is personal and can vary (achieving financial security, supporting family, helping the team succeed, allowing self-expression).

- **Impact:** The results of one's work, the subjective judgment that your work is making a difference, is important for teams. Seeing that one's work is contributing to the organization's goals can help reveal impact.[43]

Note that both Edmonson's and Google's research identified psychological safety as the most critical factor for team success. Psychological safety creates an atmosphere (culture) that allows the truth to be told without negative repercussions. Such psychological safety can vary within teams and organizations. Moreover, research shows that we prefer warmth and trustworthiness over competence any day. According to Edmonson, these are the benefits of psychological safety:

- Encourages people to speak up

- Enables clarity of thought

- Supports productive conflict

- Mitigates failure

- Promotes innovation

- Removes obstacles to success

- Increases accountability.

Leaders create psychological safety by being approachable, showing the limits of his/her knowledge, displaying fallibility, inviting participation, noting failures as learning opportunities, using direct language, setting boundaries, and holding people accountable for transgressions.[44] In short, by being vulnerable themselves, leaders encourage a safe and healthy culture in which people and teams thrive.

Vulnerability

Leaders need to establish an environment where it is safe to be vulnerable, and leaders create a culture by their behavior. To have a productive team culture, the people within it have to be able to express vulnerability.

Professor, researcher, and famed TED Talk speaker Dr. Brené Brown has become the queen of vulnerability! In the book *Daring Greatly*,[45] she wrote about how Teddy Roosevelt's speech, "The Man in the Arena," talks about the critic and the man fighting in the arena and how 'daring greatly' beats back the voice of the critic—our inner voice. By 'daring greatly,' we dare to try, fail, and try again. We beat back the inner critic—shame—our own personal gremlin that says, *I'm not {smart, attractive, lovable, worthy...} enough.* On the other hand, wholehearted people are willing to try to be vulnerable, to live life with courage, to connect with others, and have compassion. Brown teaches us that to be vulnerable is not a sign of weakness but one of courage. "Vulnerability is the core, the heart, the center of meaningful human experiences."

If we're not willing to be vulnerable or to fail, we will never learn, create, or innovate. Egotism and narcissism prevent us from being vulnerable. Narcissism is most often a shame-based fear of scarcity. Kids grow up thinking that if they're not great or extraordinary, they will be "less than" and unworthy of belonging. Such thinking causes shame, comparison, and disengagement—a dangerous trifecta. Then, they compensate by building a wall around their shame—trying to project confidence, which is the opposite of how they feel. They also reject anyone who threatens that wall of self-protection. Just look around at some politicians and corporate leaders for examples of narcissistic wall building. Walls keep others out, but they also trap our shame within.

We are our own biggest critics. We often feel both guilt and shame, but there is a critical difference between the two. According to Professor Brown, guilt tells us 'I made a mistake, and I'm sorry.' However, shame sends the message: 'I AM a mistake.' We're wired to be connected, and shame is fear of losing that connection. Only sociopaths don't have shame! We often lose our courage to do the right thing in order to preserve social acceptance. Shame categories include body image, money, work, parenting, health, sex, aging, and religion. Based on neuroscience research, we now know that mental pain, physical pain, and social rejection feel the same to the brain.[46]

According to Brown, to be fully engaged (wholehearted), you must be vulnerable—resilient to shame. To become shame resilient, we must name our shame and reach out to others with it—get vulnerable—and then shame dissipates. Shame hates the light of day. According to Brown, "If you put shame in a petri dish, it needs three things to grow exponentially: secrecy, silence and judgment. If you put the same amount of shame in a petri dish and douse it with empathy, it can't survive."[47]

Shame resistance comes with speaking about shame, reaching out to others, understanding shame triggers. Self-love and compassion help us greatly. Blame is a defensive shield we often put up to discharge our own discomfort. To quote Brown, "If blame is driving [the car], shame is riding shotgun."

To become shame-resilient at work, leaders need to:

- Have honest conversations

- Root out shame in teams and organizations

- Make people feel normal by giving them examples of how others also had difficulty

- Teach people how to give honest, constructive, and engaged feedback

Safety and Health

In his book *Leaders Eat Last,* author, TED Talk speaker, and leadership guru Simon Sinek asked the question: What makes the US Marines so great? Answer: Officers take care of their troops—always. For example, they always "eat last" after the troops. Soldiers act better than most of us because they are willing to sacrifice themselves in service of the safety of the team and other soldiers. However, Sinek observes that too often in business, leaders eat first—get paid more and stand first in line for benefits. However, great leaders put others first. They protect others. An excellent team and organization have a culture of empathy that protects and serves its people first. However, when people feel unsafe and unprotected by leaders, they feel stress and anxiety. Under such uncertainty, they seek safety and protection in silos and engage in internal politics, which hurts the organization. When we compete between those silos, we give off selfish chemicals; but when we collaborate, we give off selfless ones, allowing us to be our best selves.[48]

Sinek offers the simple, but powerful concept: The "circle of safety." In short, strong cultures provide internal protection from external threats. Weak cultures do the opposite and create toxic work environments. Intimidation, isolation, and politics inside organizations with weak cultures can be a serious threat to success. Real leaders protect the tribe from both internal and external threats. Sinek references Steve Pressfield who wrote about how the Spartans (Greek warriors) protected each other: "A warrior carries helmet and breastplate for his own protection, but his shield for the safety of the whole line [team]."⁴⁹ Without protection, factions (corporate gangs) and silos form for self-protection and ultimately hurt the entire organization. Gallup studies show that 40% of employees will quit if ignored by their bosses, and 22% leave if actively criticized. About 33% of all workers want to leave their job.⁵⁰

Sinek posits that when people feel safe at work, they band together to fight the outside competition. When they don't feel safe, they expend much energy on self-protection. Size also matters: The optimal size of a company or a working location (office/plant) would be about 150 people—Dunbar's number.⁵¹

Selfish Chemicals

Sinek explains that self-focused chemicals like dopamine, adrenaline, and cortisol drive us to "hunt," achieve, and compete to win. Dopamine gets released when we reach a goal, cross it off our to-do list, and achieve something. Feeling a sense of progress and reward is created by dopamine. Unfortunately, email, texting, overworking, gambling, alcohol and drugs can also cause the release of dopamine and become addictive, destructive habits. In an overly performance-driven environment, dopamine can become destructive to the circle of safety by creating stress, breaking down loyalty, and hurting the organization. Cortisol prepares our bodies and muscles for fight or flight. This hormone protects the body under stress. It's only intended to surge to protect in the moment. Lingering levels of cortisol—caused by difficult bosses, layoffs, and internal politics—break down the immune system, increase aggression, impair cognitive ability, and lower our capacity for empathy.

Selfless Chemicals

Selfless chemicals, such as serotonin and oxytocin, are the social glue that holds the culture together. They are "the backbone of the circle of safety."[52]

Supportive family, friends, and even coworkers get us through good and bad times by causing us to produce serotonin, a mood enhancer given off after we receive the support that makes us feel grateful towards those people. Also, generosity and physical contact like shaking hands and giving hugs stimulate oxytocin. Oxytocin boosts our immune system and makes us less addictive. Social support and recognition make us more human. In safe environments, oxytocin is given off and creates a feeling of love, friendship, belonging, and trust. A good tribe should stimulate serotonin and oxytocin (making us feel safe), not dopamine, adrenaline, and cortisol (making us feel threatened and competitive). Leaders who sacrifice for the group are revered as alphas; their followers want to follow them. Safety yields trust, and trust is the lubricant of good, responsive business.

What Real Leaders Do

- Protect—keep people safe; connect—socially bind the group; and project a vision of the future

- Break the rules only to do the right thing, never for personal gain

- Provide political and social cover from above

- Avoid "destructive abstraction" by putting a human face on statistics, not mindlessly employing draconian policies for the sake of numbers—selfish vs. selfless pursuits

- Sacrifice for the greater good of others

CONNECTED

Being connected to each other in teams and organizations is an evolutionary need. To survive, we need each other. While today that might not seem as fundamental as when we roamed the plains in tribes, consider how many people—from family to public services—support you in your life.

PURPOSEFUL

CONNECTED

SAFE

In his book *Social: Why our Brains are Wired to Connect,* social psychologist and neuroscientist Matthew Lieberman explains how our brains relate to the social world. His big message is that our social brain is every bit as important as our analytical brain—even more so. After experiments using functional magnetic resonance imaging (FMRI) studies, the author makes the following points:

- Dependence: As mammals, we're born dependent on our mothers for survival. Indeed, the social brain is embedded from birth.

- Mentalizing: We think about what others around us are thinking to not only survive but also to thrive.

- Social Pain: Both social and physical pain register in the same part of the brain.

- Teaching and Leading: To get better at teaching and leading, we need to engage our social brain to have a much better chance at success.[53]

Along with Lieberman, there is a host of social scientists, including the "big guns" like Maslow and Herzberg, who were the first to introduce us to the importance of social connection and thriving. There will be more discussion on these two scientists in the section on purpose.

In his book, *Thrive by Design: The Neuroscience that Drives High-Performance Cultures,* author and leadership expert Don Rheem notes that, as a species, humans are compelled to work together on teams and human survival has always depended on teams. For example, early hunter-gatherers were only able to survive by taking down large animals or by farming large areas with teams of people. In today's high-pressure, competitive workplace, we require that same kind of connection and teamwork to survive and compete. As herd animals, we need to feel connected. The author concludes that a great job in the future will be more about how it feels than how much it pays.[54]

So, creating conditions that sustain motivation, provide meaning, and instill trusted relationships will produce high-performance cultures. Thus, valid regular feedback and recognition of people on the team make individuals and the team stronger and higher performing.

What Leaders Can Do

- **Sit people in teams close to each other.** People need to be in proximity to create connection. Social connection comes from informal interactions. "Studies done on propinquity (proximity) indicate that because of proximity, people in apartment buildings who lived near the elevator knew statistically far more people than others."[55]

- **Encourage social events with the team.** It's a good idea to get the team together outside of the office to connect in a different way. For example, when a company decided to move away from paper coffee cups for environmental reasons, one leader took her team offsite to make and decorate team mugs, serving both environmental and team connection goals.

- **Treat team meetings like tribal councils.** Let people come together to have a voice and make team decisions. The research around action learning demonstrates the effectiveness of this technique beyond a doubt.[56]

Now, let's look at the final element of culture.

PURPOSEFUL

Which came first, the chicken or the egg? You've heard this expression before. Here's the culture equivalent: Which comes first, meaning or purpose? Because they're so closely braided together in our lives, especially relative to work, we'll explore the

most current distinctions between them. Today, purpose seems to get the nod in the lexicon but meaning is sneaking up on it.

A quote that is often attributed to Shakespeare or Picasso is actually from a psychiatrist and writer named David Viscott. In his book, *Finding Your Strength in Difficult Times,*[57] he wrote:

The purpose of life is to discover your gift. The work of life is to develop it. The meaning of life is to give your gift away.

Moreover, when it comes to finding meaning in your life, researchers have some distinct and related ideas. In her book *The Progress Principle,*[58] Harvard researcher Teresa Amabile wrote that progress toward meaningful work every day is what people seek. And, small wins get to meaningful progress. Find meaning in your life by using your talents to help others, not just seeking happiness focused on yourself. According to her research, people who lack meaning in their lives express a gene pattern that activates an inflammatory response, which can become chronic. However, people with meaning in their lives show no such gene expression.[59]

What about purpose? It is the cornerstone for psychologists Abraham Maslow and Frederick Herzberg, two motivation giants. Maslow called purpose self-actualization—when we get a chance to fully develop and use our talents. Herzberg's research found that motivation comes from our intrinsic values like recognition, respect, and impact, not from extrinsic rewards and money. People who performed purposeful work, even outside of their jobs, performed even better at work.

In her research, Professor Linda Hill at the Harvard Business School notes that successful, innovative, adaptive companies and teams have a strong shared common purpose. They get to that purpose by answering two important questions: Why do we exist, and where are we headed? A collective, overarching purpose unites people and teams. Such a vision is not just set by the leader. It also bubbles up from the bottom. Shared purpose creates the atmosphere to thrive.[60]

In his book, *The Culture Code,* Dan Coyle explained that purpose-driven questions are "What is this [work] all about, and why are we doing what we do?" Purpose is about the higher calling of work—not about the what or the how of work. Purpose is about the why of it. Teams can establish purpose by developing and enforcing priorities—especially in collective relationships. Also, he adds that leaders should support proficiency and creativity separately but equally, develop memorable culture slogans, measure what matters most, develop symbols (artifacts) of culture, and set the behavior bar high and with specific, defined actions.[61]

Professor Clay Christenson is regarded as one of the country's leading experts on innovation and growth. The author of many books, such as *The Innovator's DNA, Competing Against Luck,* and *The Innovator's Dilemma,* he is also very well known for *How Will You Measure Your Life?* which was developed from an exercise he conducts on the last day of his class at Harvard. In this exercise, Christensen applies the theories the class studied all semester to the students' lives. He lists the theories on the board. Then he asks three powerful questions. How can I be sure that... 1) I will be successful and happy in my career? 2) [in] my relationships with my spouse, my children and my extended family and close friends, I become an enduring source of happiness? 3) I live a life of integrity and stay out of jail? Christensen, himself an HBS grad, has seen classmates like Jeff Skilling, former Enron CEO, end up in jail. The essence of this book is that if, at work and in our personal lives, we find a purpose (both individually and collectively as part of a team), commit ourselves to that purpose, and measure ourselves against that purpose, our chances of achieving happiness and avoiding bad outcomes are greatly increased.[62]

The Netflix Culture

As the Chief Talent Officer at Netflix, Patty McCord along with CEO Reed Smith helped build the culture at Netflix. She produced the Netflix Culture Deck, which has been viewed online over fifteen million times. Facebook's Sheryl Sandberg called the deck one of the most important documents to ever come out of Silicon Valley. Now, McCord has written what amounts to a corporate culture memoir, *Powerful: Building a Culture of Freedom and Responsibility.*[63]

Netflix practiced "incremental adaptation" by innovating, failing, and learning. Eventually, a great culture emerged that allowed Netflix to grow and remain competitive in a survival-of-the-fittest world. Distilling their core cultural values and injecting them into people, and especially teams, effectively fueled Netflix's successful strategy. Creating positive cultural conditions that allow great teams to do great work is the essential responsibility of management.

According to McCord, management must recruit the best talent, empower people and teams, and get rid of policies and procedures that get in the way. "Rapid disruption" assumes that everything changes; so, it's good to embrace a culture of innovative team problem-solving. To transform their culture, Netflix developed core values and identified specific behaviors and disciplines to ensure that people execute on them. Such behaviors included: Open and clear communication, radical honesty, fact-based opinions, customer- and company-centric decision-making, managing teams with integrity and responsibility, and modeling good behavior. Eventually, the famed

Netflix Culture Deck was developed and widely distributed as the Netflix cultural manifesto.

Current Research:
Meaning, Purpose, and Significance

Professors Michael Steger and Laura King helped us refine our notions of meaning, purpose, and significance.

According to Steger in his TED Talk, meaning is comprised of purpose and significance.[64] Specifically, purpose represents "… an anchor we throw out into the future," a dream we pursue. It operates like a beacon that beckons us.

However, we live in a day-to-day world of "getting and spending" as the poet William Wordsworth said in his poem "The World Is Too Much With Us."

The world is too much with us; late and soon,

Getting and spending, we lay waste our powers;

So, how do we find this grand thing we call purpose in the daily grind of the world of "getting and spending?" According to Steger's research, in such a reality, meaning evolves to take a front-row seat, ahead of the more elusive long-view—purpose. In fact, we find meaning in the smallest events in our lives (a sunrise, the touch of a child, a kind word, a wink, and virtually anything we do as humans interacting with the world, especially other people) through the concept of significance.

Steger contends that our purpose (our long-term anchor), supported by our day-to-day significant events, weave together to give our lives meaning. Thus, if your purpose in life is to serve the world as a teacher, you will find meaning whenever a student has an ah-ha, insightful moment. Truly, there's nothing like it when students "get it." Your life as a teacher is infused by significance—watching a student respond.

In an experiment, college students were told to go out and take pictures of things that make their lives feel meaningful. Ninety percent of the students brought back pictures of people. As Steger puts it, "...relationships are the ocean in which we find meaning."

How important is meaning?

Patricia Boyle, PhD, study co-author and associate professor of behavioral sciences at the Rush University Medical Center in Chicago, has found that mental health, and especially positive psychological factors such as having a purpose in life, are very potent determinants of health outcomes. Dr. Boyle's research on senior adults showed that having a strong sense of purpose in life could serve as an antidote to strokes and damage that precedes dementia and even Alzheimer's.[65] "Clinicians need to be aware of patients' mental state and encourage behaviors that will increase purpose and other positive emotional states." Worth noting, we're all motivated by purpose differently, so finding what motivates us is important.[66]

Special Note: See the section of this book about values to help find your key motivators that will lead to purposeful life.

Like Steger, Professor Laura King teaches psychology at the University of Missouri and focuses on personality, well-being, and meaning. She's written and spoken extensively on the distinction between meaning, purpose, and significance. Like Steger, her research leads her to view meaning as the big kahuna of happiness. Moreover, she views meaning as a combination of purpose, a longer-term anchor in our lives, and significance, the value we put on daily activities, big and small, as they add context in our lives. In short, her formula for a meaningful life is the following: Meaning = Significance + Purpose. In a particularly lucid presentation, she makes several important insights.[67]

While the research about purpose and meaning is evolving, we conclude that both working in concert together offer high value in our lives. Thus, having a long-term anchor in our lives can drive and sustain us. Also, daily events give our lives meaning, context, and significance. So, paying attention to daily meaningful events while also developing a long-term sense of purpose in our lives will likely make us feel fulfilled and happy.

Consider the collective effect when entire teams and organizations have meaning—significance and purpose. Look at the education field, which regrettably is one of the lower-paid professions. When you find a team of teachers working collectively on improving the curriculum or working together on a team project to help students in need, there are very few job offers—regardless of salary—that would take them away from their meaningful work life. Police officers enjoy that same sense of purpose and meaning, especially when working on SWAT teams, investigative teams, or forensic teams where everyone is focused on enforcing the law and protecting the public. Again, money is not the differentiator when it comes to having a meaningful profession. Rather, it's the mission and the team's focus on both day-to-day significant experiences, like a thank you or smile from a citizen who's been helped, and a deep sense of purpose, as expressed in the often-heard law enforcement mantra of "protect and serve." Understanding how we make meaning—individually, as a team, and as an organization—separates the high functioning from the rest.

05: STRATEGY

Engaged, motivated people and a trusted leader, all operating in an excellent culture, are still not quite enough for high-performance teams. There's one final critical element: strategy. Everyone on the team must also be committed to rowing the boat in the same direction in order to achieve team results. That calls for a solid team strategy—

Figure 14 The Team Leadership Pyramid: Strategy

the rudder of the high performing team. Strategies can be overly complex as you might see in larger organizations. At the basic level in teams, it boils down to fundamental questions—Why? What? How? —as suggested by experienced organizational and leadership experts like Simon Sinek.[68] Team strategy completes The Team Leadership Pyramid and consists of three levels or planks that answer the three fundamental questions:

- Why do we exist?—our mission, vision, and values

- What do we need to do get to our why?—our goals

- How do we accomplish our goals to ultimately deliver on the vision—our objectives?

All teams exist within a larger organizational context. We can't isolate teams from organizations without doing injustice to both. No matter how basic an organization may seem, the best ones are always driven by fundamental beliefs—not just by revenue. Sure, money matters. But the reasons people join a business are driven by more fundamental "why" questions like mission, vision, and values. Also, teams—like nested dolls—fit within a larger context. They reflect and support the larger organizational strategy—mission, vision, values, goals, and objectives—while, at the same time, also crafting their own team strategies. So, let's get started.

First, we'll discuss the basic strategy triangle, then, how to develop a team strategy and, finally, how to enhance team performance through coaching.

COMPONENTS OF TEAM STRATEGY

When trying to understand that an organization is a team of teams, it is important to keep in mind the notion that, as previously mentioned, teams are nested within organizations. They share, amplify, and focus the organization's strategy. Nonetheless, to become a great team, the fundamental questions about team mission, vision, and values need to be asked.

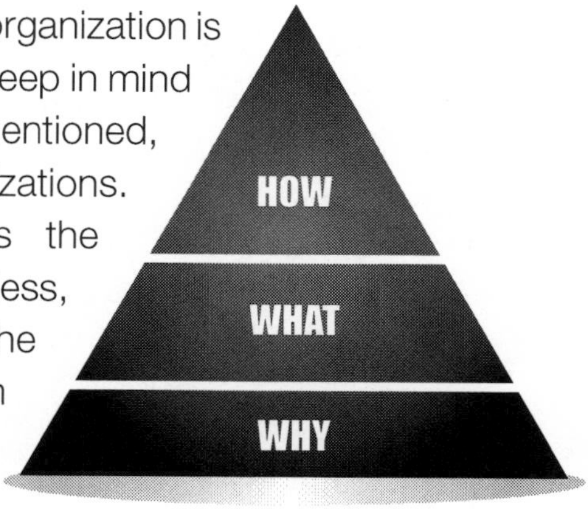

Figure 15 The Strategy Triangle

Why

Mission: Why does the team exist?

With this question, we consider the team's most foundational value to the organization. Why does the sales team, the marketing team, or the communications team exist? If the team did not exist, would it have to be established? Often, as companies grow and change, some teams continue to answer this question well. Those teams remain relevant. In other cases, changes in the industry landscape may have made certain teams irrelevant. For example, the electric-typewriter division at IBM morphed into a very different team as technology changed the landscape. For companies and organizations, the answer to "Why" should generally be more stable and fundamental—but always subject to adaptation.

Vision: What does the team aspire to become or deliver in the future?

When it comes to moving the team forward, we'll need to consider the vision of its leader, informed by those who are closest to the work. A big mistake teams and organizations make is to focus only on today. While mindfulness tells us to be in the moment, leaders must also consider the future direction of their teams and organizations. To project the future, organizational leaders need to talk to all relevant stakeholder groups, such as employees, customers, partners and investors. Team leaders need to talk to team members, adjacent teams, internal and external customers, and relevant groups.

The classic set of questions to ask center around S.W.O.T.— What are our internal team **strengths** and **weaknesses?** What are the external team **opportunities** and **threats?** This simple, effective series of questions provides a consistent evaluative framework for companies and organizations. Once you answer the S.W.O.T. team questions, the data begins to point in a particular direction. Then, the question remains: What will we look like in one to three years? That's the vision. In years past, we projected ahead five, even ten years. However, the hyper development of technology has blown up that time frame. So, we must adapt to a new time horizon.

Values: What values or principles will guide the team?

Every sailor knows the value of the north star—it's the reference point for any kind of nautical navigation. Same thing with values. While the focus of the company might change, values should be consistent and act as a guiding star. Consider the values of the FBI (Federal Bureau of Investigation) which have remained consistent over time: Fidelity, Bravery, and Integrity. While the FBI has adapted many times to a changing culture and priorities, those fundamental values have remained steadfast. Every team of agents in every city in the US lives by those values every day. Anyone who violates them is held strictly accountable. Keep team values focused, easy to understand, congruent with organizational values, and enforce them vigorously. Hire and fire based on them.

What

Goals: What are the interdependent goals?

After answering the why questions, teams will need to answer the what

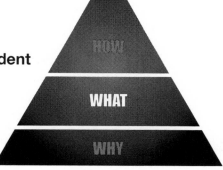

question. What will you do to fulfill your why—your mission, vision, and values? Notice how when the why is clear, the what becomes much easier, which is the reason that the why question needs to get answered first.

The foundational requirements for good teams include: bounded, we know who's really on the team; stable, the team stays intact; and interdependent, to get things done, they have to depend on each other.[69] So, it is with goals. They need to be bounded, clearly focused, and stable. We stick with them until they're accomplished or modified. Finally, to be effective, goals need to require interdependent action.

Relevance: How do they relate directly back to the Why?

Let's take a senior team leadership goal, like "Developing a company-wide leadership development program for high potential leaders." That kind of goal will drive more passion, action, and unity than a goal like, "Expanding the market by 10%." Goals are broad-based pillars of the company's mission and vision. They provide specifics that lead to even finer points as expressed by objectives. In a broad sense, if goals were part of a GPS system, the mission and vision would be the destination (where you are heading and why). The goals would show the major highways (the high-level directions and milestones to be reached along the way). The objectives would show the close details (the turn-by-turn steps along the route).

How

Objectives: What are the specific steps needed to achieve the goals and how will we measure success?

As alluded to, objectives are where the team strategy rubber meets the road. Objectives answer the question: How do we get the job done?

Critical objectives are those that lead to big goals being met. Simply asking the question, "If we didn't have this objective, would we get to the goal?" helps identify a critical objective. In the example about a team developing a high potential development program, does the objective "Identify the critical professional factors to consistently identify potential candidates for the program" make sense? What would happen if you could not consistently identify the best candidates? Maybe confusion, resentment, or even rejection. So, the objective stays.

Measures: How will we know if we have accomplished the objectives?

When you want to assess any objectives, think S. M. A. R. T. Specific. Measurable. Attainable. Relevant. Timebound.[70] Are the objectives specific enough so that anyone on the team would know what's expected? So, an objective like "Understand how to recruit new candidates" isn't specific or clear enough. Whereas, "Develop the specific criteria to assess and select people for the high potential program and deliver to the executive leadership team for review by January 20." With agreement that this objective is attainable by January 20, you have the basis for a S.M.A.R.T. objective. So, how does this all come together for a team? Let's take a look at the steps for developing a team strategy.

DEVELOPING A TEAM STRATEGY

There are two distinct times in the life cycle of a team where developing a team strategy typically occurs.

- **Launching a New Team**: When a new team is being formed, it is like starting from a blank slate. A new team could be a new project that is kicking off, a new management team that is being formed, or a significant membership change to a team.

- **Relaunching an Existing Team:** Oftentimes, existing teams must come together to deal with issues interfering with their performance or to enhance effectiveness in the future. At that time, there is an opportunity to step back and 'relaunch' the team to bring everyone back into alignment.

Launch/Relaunch Meeting

Bringing the new team or the existing team together for a formal launch/relaunch is a critical step for developing the team strategy and getting the team started off on the right foot. Research has found that it accounts for a significant 30% of the team's ongoing success. So, it is essential for it to be effective. [71]

There are several things to keep in mind when scheduling the launch meeting.

- Plan for the meeting to be offsite for full focus on the important business of launching/relaunching the team.

- Ensure that only the clearly identified team members are invited and that they can all be present. If even one team member can't attend, look to find a better date as everyone's input and alignment is critical.

- Consider using an experienced team coach to facilitate this important meeting. This is not coaching per se but coach-facilitation. Thus, the coach asks questions and controls the flow and the timing. The coach explains her/his role as the facilitator of the meeting and the rules of the day.

- Confirm that everyone knows the importance of the meeting and its main objective—to develop a *team* strategic plan, not an *organizational* strategic plan. Of course, both strategies are connected, but high-functioning teams have their own distinct team strategy. This strategy-within-a strategy sometimes confuses people early on, so beware.

Key Components of a Launch/Relaunch Meeting

The launch/relaunch meeting agenda should consist of the following components in the order shown below:

- Connection

- Purpose

- Teamwork

- Plan

Connection

It is important that team members know and understand each other. Consider taking a personality or individual-style instrument before the meeting. Then, share and discuss the results at the start of the launch meeting to give everyone a baseline understanding of each other's style, how they work, and their preferred method of communication. A good team coach/facilitator can help make this a very productive, even fun conversation.

Sample assessments that are free to everyone online include:

- Various personality assessments at www.123test.com to determine cognitive types, styles, and preferences

- VIA Character Strengths online assessment at www.viacharacter.org to understand individual character strengths

Spend the time to find connection points across the team, like common interests or common experiences, and let people uncover things about each other that they may not have known before. For example, a fun way to kick off the meeting is to ask everyone to go around the table and introduce themselves, tell their role on the team, and share one interesting/odd/funny thing about themselves that their teammates would not likely know. It gets people connecting, learning, laughing, and talking right up front. It sets everyone at ease.

Make sure to capture the name of each person and each person's role & responsibilities on the team, even if the individuals know each other. This information will be included in the Team Charter document—a concise summary of the why, what, and how of a team that serves as a strategic anchor and reference for the future.

Purpose

A large chunk of the time should be dedicated to this important section—the purpose. It is important to have each team member contribute to this discussion and for the team to negotiate together to align on a common mission and vision.

- Mission: Why does the team exist? What is its purpose?

- Vision: What does the team aspire to become or deliver in the future?

Let's look at a couple of examples.

A software development project team

For a project team brought together to launch a new software to the company's users, a sample mission might be:

To design, build, and implement the 'xyz' software solution that connects teams virtually across the enterprise.

A sample vision of that same team might be something like:

To become a high performing team that delivers top-notch software solutions to the organization in an effective and efficient manner.

An Internal HR team

An example of a mission statement for a Human Resources team might be:

To support the organization's success through people, policies, and procedures that contribute to a diverse, safe, and healthy work environment.

A sample vision of that same team might be something like:

Our team's vision is to be recognized as a high-caliber provider of innovative HR services that supports our employees throughout their tenure.

Teamwork

As noted already, great teamwork comes about when there are great people, leaders, culture, and strategy. As research has demonstrated, both a strong set of values and a set of team norms will keep teamwork on track, especially during difficult times.

Values

The team should develop a shared set of team values they agree to exhibit and hold each other accountable to the values. Simply put: What values or principles will be the guiding lights/ north star principles for the team?

Here are a few examples of values a team might select:

Honesty	Reliability
Trust	Efficiency
Transparency	Quality
Diversity	Accountability
Innovation	Customer Service

You can find a plethora of lists of possible values online if the team struggles with coming up with some on their own. These sample lists can serve as a starting point to get the dialogue moving.

Team Working Agreements

Another important component is developing a list of shared team working agreements — team norms. This is a list of agreements or behavioral norms that the team commits to upholding. Agreements can include things as simple as being present and on time for all meetings, or more complex, such as how the team agrees to handle conflicts. Sometimes the team coach/facilitator will need to help get the team started on identifying these agreements. Then, the team will pick up the momentum and start generating agreements on its own.

Here are just a few team working agreement examples:

- Make team meetings top priority

- Start and end meetings on time

- Communicate in advance if a deliverable will not be met and why (no surprises)

- Issues must be addressed with the person directly before being escalated

- No cell phones on the table during team meetings

- If you must miss a meeting where decisions will be made, send in your thoughts to the team leader in advance

- Agree to disagree and disagree respectfully

- Work to find the solution — no blame game

- Accept personal responsibility for your behavior and your deliverables

Plan

Once the team why is firmly established, the team must plan what it needs to accomplish and how it will go about getting things done.

What

The team coach/facilitator will take the team through the important steps of developing the team strategy as outlined earlier in this chapter. Based on the mission, the team will start by identifying the interdependent goals they must accomplish as a collaborative, interdependent team—the what.

Some examples of team goals are:

- Design, build, and deliver the new CRM system to the sales team by April 1

- Improve the team's close rate by 15% in 2020

- Successfully transition the organization to the new enterprise platform by October 15

- Reduce order intake errors by 25% in 2020

- Launch new hire onboarding process in Q2

How

After the S.M.A.R.T. (Specific. Measurable. Attainable. Relevant. Timebound.) goals have been solidified, the team will work through the plan to achieve them—the how. These are the team objectives. The coach/facilitator will work with the team to establish the specific objectives—the steps that must be achieved to keep the team on track to meet the overarching goals. For example, if a customer service team has a goal of reducing order intake errors by 25% in one year, a few objectives might include:

- Complete a root cause analysis of order intake errors by May 1

- Automate customer look up information in online order form by June 15

- Develop and deliver enhanced order intake training to customer service representatives by October 1

The expectation is that achieving each of these objectives would move the team closer to accomplishing the overall goal. The team would also agree on how they would measure whether the objectives were accomplished.

After the plan has been developed by the team, the coach/ facilitator takes all the information collected and creates the Team Charter — a concise summary of the why, what, and how of a team. The Team Charter is shared with the team electronically to review and discussed in depth at the follow-up meeting where the team will modify and/or adjust as needed.

As a reminder of what a sample Team Charter might look like, below is the sample shared in the Case Study in Part 2 of this book.

OGC Leadership Development Team Charter

The Why:

- **Mission**: Our team exists to develop, deliver, and evaluate high-performance leadership development programs for OGC — specifically for both first-line and high potential leaders.
- **Vision**: To be considered the gold standard for our focus on leadership development in government contracting by an outside assessor — like the Association for Talent Development (ATD) or the Society for Human Resource Management (SHRM).
- **Values**: Transparency, Collaboration, Trust
- **Working Agreements**:
  - Be present (cell phones off and away unless needed for an exercise)
  - Fight fair (no name-calling or ganging up on anyone)
  - Bring your A-Game (come to meetings prepared)
  - Protect the team (when you leave a meeting, no bad-mouthing anyone)

The What:

- Develop a 6-month training curriculum for first-line managers by July 1, and
- Develop a 1-year training curriculum for high potential leaders by October 1

The How:

Goals and Objectives

	GOALS	MEASURE(S)
1	**Develop a 6-month training curriculum for first-line managers by July 1**	• Conduct research on existing programs from similar organizations by February 15 • Complete an internal competency assessment for first-line leaders by March 31 • Develop and test curriculum by June 15 • Senior management review and approval by July 1
2	**Develop a 1-year training curriculum for high potential leaders by October 1**	• Identify core competency elements in discussion with senior leadership by February 1 • Evaluate off-the-shelf content options and consultant resources by March 1 • Identify subject matter experts for key topics by April 15 • Each subject matter expert to work with existing content and consultant resources to develop training module and workbook by September 1 • Review curriculum and training plan with Executive Committee by October 1

DELIVERING ON THE TEAM STRATEGY

Once the team strategy has been developed and documented in the Team Charter, it needs to be executed. It should be a living, breathing tool, and not something that sits on the shelf gathering dust. Establishing a routine review is key to keeping the strategy front and center. This will ensure progress and accountability.

Monthly Team Sessions

We recommend monthly sessions facilitated by a team coach (internal or external) that would consist of two elements: Progress Checks and Ongoing Team Problem Solving.

Part 1 - Progress Check

The first part of the meeting should be solely focused on the Team Charter document. Each goal and objective should be assessed to check progress. A visual stoplight dashboard indicator can be helpful for tracking progress toward the goals by marking them with one of the three stoplight colors: green = on track to meet the schedule, yellow = at risk of meeting the schedule, red = significantly at risk of meeting the schedule. Each of the objectives and assigned tasks is reviewed to hold all team members accountable while also providing visibility to all team members into progress and potential impacts. The team may need to renegotiate activities, timelines or resources required. Again, the team strategy is a living, breathing tool. The team will also discuss upcoming priorities for the month and confirm if they are still on track. The coach will facilitate this conversation and keep track of the progress and the agreements. This section of the session usually takes between 45- 60 minutes.

Part 2 - Team Problem Solving

During these monthly sessions, the second half should be allocated to conducting a team problem-solving coaching session. Often before this session, each participant is asked to identify one or two problems facing the *entire team*. The team-wide issues are captured then prioritized to identify the most pressing issue.

Below, you'll find a list of key players, the rules, and a description of the process.

- Team Coach: The coach facilitates the process. S/he can direct questions, clarify, and comment on the process but does not directly try to solve the problem for participants.

- Participants: Four to eight people works best. If you have fewer than four people, you'll lose the power of cognitive diversity—people thinking differently about the same problem. With more than eight people, you'll have trouble just getting the meeting to happen, and the complexities of intergroup relationships multiply geometrically.

- Rules:

  ➢ The coach can stop and start the meeting at any time.

  ➢ Participants may only speak if responding to a direct question from another participant or the coach.

  ➢ Anyone can ask anyone else in the group a question.

- Questions: They should be open and information-seeking. Questions like Who, What, How, When, and even Why are best.

- Process: Using the Coach-Approach process works well—Problem, Present, Possible, and Plan.

- Steps: This is the sequence of the problem-solving session.

  ➤ The protocol is for the coach to remind everyone in the group about the three simple (but powerful) rules of coaching—see above.

  ➤ Next, the coach pulls out or draws the Coach-Approach on the board as a roadmap for decision making.

  ➤ The coach begins by asking the problem owner to give a brief overview (5 minutes or less) of the problem s/he faces. The best problems are ones that apply to the entire team and are interdependent.

  ➤ The coach asks who has the first question about the problem. Then, the coach monitors the group—insuring that people stick to curiosity, ask questions, and refrain from giving answers. Especially restrain them from acting like consultants and offering solutions before the group figures out what the real problem is.

  ➤ Think-Write-Share: To ensure that introverts express their thoughts and to keep extraverts from dominating the conversation, giving time for each person to write down their responses can be very effective. Then, each person is asked to share one thought. The process is repeated until all thoughts and ideas have been voiced.

> Coach-directed questions: The coach asks follow-up questions of the team. For example, the coach may ask, "So what's the problem?" and then let them talk, especially with common team problems.

> Worth noting: Most of the problems or issues that are initially raised rarely turn out to be the actual problem, rather the symptom of the dysfunction that gets uncovered by good coaching.

> Accountability: After each of the questions in the problem-solving model has been asked and answered and there appears to be a clear starting point reached in the plan moving forward, the coach will ask what the team will do first, who will be accountable for each particular task, when it will get done, and how the group will know it has been done. Thus, there is strict accountability for action. Coaching helps to drive change.

> Next meeting: At the following meeting, the coach asks for people to report the results of their ongoing efforts. Following their responses, the coach solicits whether the team charter needs ongoing refinement on the next steps or to address another key issue or problem. Thus, the process is ongoing.

As you can see, each team meeting is both a strategic accountability session and a problem-solving session that helps the team move forward toward their goals. Teams find this process to be an effective use of their time as they learn how to operate better as a team.

Additionally, we've found that coaching the team leader individually is essential and coaching her/his team simultaneously is the most effective way to ensure high performing teams. Otherwise, the coach never sees the results of coaching in context—where the rubber meets the road—within the working of the team. The coaching cadence works best when the leader and coach meet once or twice a month and the team meets every month in the beginning to keep up the momentum. Make no mistake, quarterly or biannual meetings are helpful but don't keep up the momentum necessary for high performing teams. You may recall from the beginning of the book that only 20% of teams are high performing.

06: THE 6 CONDITIONS FOR TEAM SUCCESS

As discussed in the previous chapter on team strategy, teams can be newly formed or they can be existing teams that need a relaunch to clarify purpose and gain alignment. It is important to continuously review the performance of the team to ensure there are no barriers to success. Both scenarios benefit from a team assessment to ensure the teams are functioning well together and to identify any potential areas that might need to be addressed. For new teams, it is best to wait several months before doing an assessment, so the team has enough time to work together to collect valuable data. However, for existing teams that are coming together because of issues identified, it is important to start first with an assessment of the team to understand the root causes of its ineffectiveness. The team will work together to address those areas, ideally with a trained coach/facilitator, and then move to the step of developing the team strategy, which results in the Team Charter.

Assessing the Team

Extensive research on teams has been conducted by Richard Hackman and Ruth Wageman at Harvard. Their research showed that few teams, especially executive teams, are high performing. After decades of assessing teams in diverse industries, they discovered that as few as one in five teams is high performing. Hackman and Wageman identified a set of three essential and three enabling conditions that must exist for a team to be successful. From this research, they developed the Team Diagnostic Survey (TDS™) that collects data from the team around these six success conditions. We have determined that the 6 Conditions research affirms and reflects many of our findings, amplifies their impact, and lays a solid, valid and reliable foundation for high performing teams.

The Process

A coach trained on the TDS™ will help facilitate this process. The team is directed to complete the online TDS™ survey. After the survey results have been collected, the coach compiles all the collected information and shares it with the team leader. The leader reviews the insights and works with the coach to begin to think about which areas to address with the team first. A separate meeting with the team is held to focus specifically on the results of this activity. If this is an existing team needing a relaunch, this assessment and up-front meeting would occur before a relaunch meeting to ensure the team is working on addressing the core issues.

SURVEY MEASURES/
SUCCESS CONDITIONS

The TDS™ survey is focused on the three essential and three enabling conditions that make teams work. These six foundational conditions influence team task functions in three key areas: effort, strategy, and knowledge & skills. Ensuring a solid foundation sets the team up for greater effectiveness, as measured by member satisfaction, quality of group process, and task performance. Once you have these six conditions and three efforts present, launching the team strategically will ensure a high performing team. Let's examine at those essential and enabling conditions that the Team Diagnostic Survey will assess.

Essential Conditions

- **Real Team:** Teams are bounded, interdependent, and stable.

  - ➤ Bounded: Everyone knows who is on the team. It's surprising how often that is unclear. Each person must be critical to the team's mission and strategy.

  - ➤ Interdependent: Team members work toward a common purpose in a way that they interact and share common resources to succeed. They depend on each other—no silos.

  - ➤ Stable: Talent turnover is anathema to high performance. Teams must be together long enough to know and rely on members' strengths and different perspectives.

- **Right People:** Teams must have diversity and skills equal to the team's purpose.

  - ➤ Diversity: People have different perspectives and cognitive approaches, and high performing teams take the time to make sure all are aware of each other's perspectives.

  - ➤ Skills: People have the right skills required— including teamwork skills and experience. Skills must match the team's needs.

- **Compelling Purpose:** Teams have a purpose that is challenging, clear, and consequential.

➢ Challenging: The team's purpose must be a stretch to push the team but not be a bridge so far that the team gets discouraged.

➢ Clear: Members must be able to visualize what the purpose looks like.

➢ Consequential: The purpose must have a meaningful and significant impact on the lives of others and make the world a better place.

Enabling Conditions

- **Sound Structure:** To tackle problems, teams need solid task design, size, and team behavioral norms.

  ➢ Task Design: The problem or task requires a team. Each team member's experience and judgment need to be used in the process.

  ➢ Team Size: Teams are often much too large to be effective. Research favors teams of four to eight people.

  ➢ Team Norms: Teams need rules of behavior—how they treat each other.

- **Support:** Organizational structures and systems support and promote teamwork—like rewards and recognition, information, education, and resources.

  ➢ Rewards and Recognition: Pay and recognition are for the team, not just individual achievement and performance.

- ➤ Information: The team gets useful information, on a timely basis, in a form they can use, and in a way that they can understand it.

- ➤ Education/Consultation: Teams have technical assistance available when they encounter new problems requiring more support.

- ➤ Resources: The team gets the resources needed for success—space, technology, vehicles, etc.

- **Coaching:** Finally, teams need coaching to succeed. Teams need specific team coaching, availability of the coach, and helpfulness from the coach. The coach can be internal or external. An external coach is often beneficial if there is no one trained in team coaching.

  - ➤ Team Coaching: A coach is available to the team and intervenes at significant points during team interactions.

  - ➤ Availability: Coaching is readily available to teams on a just-in-time basis.

  - ➤ Helpfulness: The coach is experienced at performing team coaching.

Ensuring these six conditions are met is the foundation for the team's success. Together, they will impact the team task processes which will, in turn, drive the overall performance of the team. These components are also measured in the TDS™ and are as follows:

Team Task Processes

The research has determined three task processes as critical to team success: **effort, strategy,** and **knowledge** & **skills.** Whenever you discover deficits in any of these three, it should be a red flag. Focus your attention back to the essential and enabling conditions for guidance. Does the team have the resources it needs? Has the need changed? Are the right people on the team?

Here's a closer look at the three task processes.

1. Effort

Whether it be an individual or team, effort can make the difference between a good or great team. How hard-working and focused is the team?

2. Strategy

Effort without direction is like a quarterback without a receiver. Strategy keeps the team on course. Poor direction leads to disengagement and failure. How effective is the team's approach to their work as a team?

3. Knowledge & Skills

Is the team leveraging the knowledge and experience of each member? Remember, when people can use their strengths most of the day, they're more engaged and happier, resulting in higher team performance.

Team Effectiveness

Assessing team effectiveness has always been elusive. However, Hackman and Wageman's research offers a clear set of criteria in three specific areas.

1. Team Task Performance

Simply put, are the key stakeholders pleased with the efforts of the team? Is the client happy with the team's progress and performance? So, if the team is supposed to develop software, how does the client rate success? If it is an executive team, how pleased is the board with their performance? One way to assess this would be to ask on a scale of 1 to 5 (1 is low and 5 is high), how pleased is the client with the team's progress/performance? If the average answer is 3.5 or below, then you will need to look back at the essential and enabling conditions for clues about how to elevate performance and progress.

2. Quality Group Process

Excellent teams get better with time and experience. Simply put, one key question to ask: Has the team functioning improved, according to the team members? Again, a simple 1-5 assessment (explained above) will reveal clues to look back to the essential and enabling conditions.

3. Team Member Satisfaction

If you consider each team member as an important team resource, then their satisfaction is critical, lest they opt off the team. The research has determined that the level of each team member's satisfaction determines the health and productivity of the team. Each team member needs to answer these questions: As a team member, have I benefited by being on this team? Have I learned and grown from the team experience? Again, a simple 1-5 assessment will reveal clues to look back to the essential and enabling conditions.

All elements of the Harvard research are pulled together into the Team Diagnostic Survey (TDS™), a valid (measures what it intends to measure) and reliable (produces consistent results) instrument to help you understand what might lead to or keep you from team success. The TDS™ acts like an "MRI of the team" that peers into the deep tissue and substance of the team—essential and enabling conditions. After the assessment, teams can then know where to focus precisely on critical team issues at monthly team-coaching meetings.

CONCLUSION

When you get to the end of a book, one of the most critical questions is: What did I learn? How will it help me in my life?

We hope that *Leading Teams* has provided you with a model for success when dealing with teams of any kind, family, work, and community. If we think of any organization as a team of teams and think of individual people like logs in a fire, whose energy only comes when they burn with the energy of other logs, then the importance of teams comes clearly into view.

We spent many hours researching the researchers and what they had to say about teams. Considering all our research, we made four conclusions about the critical elements of great teams—the Team Leadership Pyramid.

- **People.** Teams operate particularly well with people who think in diverse ways, who are engaged using both their skills and character strengths every day, and who operate autonomously.

- **Leader.** Trust is the overriding characteristic of effective leaders. Trust is composed of three critical elements: character, competence and compassion for others— the trust triangle, as we call it.

- **Culture.** For people and leaders to thrive, they need to operate in a healthy environment that is psychologically safe (people speak truth to power without fear of reprisal); connected (people feel part of a supportive tribe); and, purpose-driven (people focus on something beyond themselves—a higher purpose).

- **Strategy.** Finally, people, leaders, and culture require direction (strategy) and need to answer the questions of why we exist and where we're headed in the future. What must we do to make that happen? And how do we get that done?

We shared with you the importance of a launch/relaunch meeting to bring the team together to shape their team behaviors and path forward. During that meeting, the team will develop the team strategy and memorialize it in a Team Charter. Establishing a regular meeting cadence using team coaching to review progress is a key success factor. People need the strategy in front of them regularly to stay on course and to deliver on the priorities, and an accountability session pulls that through.

We also introduced the work of Hackman and Wageman from Harvard. Their research reveals that high performing teams have three essential conditions and three enabling conditions that when present produce results and people who are actively engaged and progressing as a team and as individuals. They also produced the Team Diagnostic Survey (TDS™) and what we believe is the most accurate "MRI of a team" that exists today. Research-driven, the TDS™ offers the most valid (measures what it promises to measure) and reliable (consistently produces the same results) team assessment tool on the market.

This research at Harvard and the 6 Conditions reflect many of *Leading Teams'* findings, amplify their impact, and provide a valid and reliable foundation for assessing and coaching high-performing teams. We openly offer all we've learned to help advance the notion of team coaching—the new frontier of coaching. We hope others will do the same.

REFERENCES

1. McChrystal, S. A., Collins, T., Silverman, D., & Fussell, C. (2015). *Team of teams: new rules of engagement for a complex world.* New York: Portfolio/Penguin.
2. Houle, D. (2008). *The shift age.* Place of publication not identified: Booksurge.
3. Gladis, S. (2010). *The trusted leader: understanding the trust triangle.* Amherst, MA: HRD Press.
4. Schein, E. H. (2016). *Organization culture and leadership.* John Wiley & Sons Inc.
5. Collins, J. (2001). *Good to great: why some companies make the leap... and others don't.* London: Random House.
6. Peters, J and Gladis, S. (2018, January) *Team coaching that accelerates performance.* TD Magazine. Retrieved from https://www.td.org/magazines/td-magazine/team-coaching-that-accelerates-performance
7. Pew Research Center. "Baby Boomers Retire." *Pew Research Center, Pew Research Center*, 7 Feb. 2014. Retrieved from https://www.pewresearch.org/fact-tank/2010/12/29/baby-boomers-retire.
8. Page, S. (2007). *The Difference: How the Power of Diversity Creates Better Groups, Firms, Schools, and Societies.* New Jersey: Princeton University Press.
9. Ibid.
10. Groupthink. Retrieved from https://www.psychologytoday.com/us/basics/groupthink
11. Ibid.
12. C. Dunlop, personal communication, May 15, 2019.
13. Marquardt, M. J., Zainuddin, A., & Yahaya, N. H. Y. (2004). *Optimizing the Power of Action Learning.* Mountain View, CA: Davies-Black Publishing.

14. Karlgaard, R., & Malone, M. S. (2015). *Team genius: the new science of high-performing organizations.* New York, NY: Harper Business.
15. C. Dunlop, personal communication, May 15, 2019.
16. Frequently Asked Questions. Retrieved from http://www.viacharacter.org/www/About-Institute/FAQs
17. Ibid.
18. Ibid.
19. Burnett, W., & Evans, D. J. (2018). *Designing your life: build a life that works for you.* London: Vintage Books.
20. Institute of Management Foundation. (1998). *Abraham Maslow: the hierarchy of needs.* Corby.
21. Herzberg, F. (2008). *One more time: how do you motivate employees?* Boston, MA: Harvard Business Press.
22. Pink, D. H. (2010). *Drive: the surprising truth about what motivates us*. Edinburgh: Canongate.
23. Gladis, S. (2017). *Leading well: becoming a mindful leader-coach.* Fairfax, VA: SGLP.
24. Marquardt, M. J., Banks, S., Cauweiler, P., & Ng, C. S. (2018). *Optimizing the power of action learning: real-time strategies for developing leaders, building teams and transforming organizations.* London: Nicholas Brealey Publishing.
25. Ibid.
26. Hougaard, R., & Carter, J. (2018). *The mind of the leader: how to lead yourself, your people, and your organization for extraordinary results.* Boston, MA: Harvard Business Review Press.
27. Rokeach, M. (1973). *The Nature of Human Values.* New York: The Free Press.
28. Gladis, S. D. (1993). *WriteType: Personality Types and Writing Styles.* Amherst, MA: HRD Press.
29. Rock, D. (2010). *Your brain at work: strategies for overcoming distraction, regaining focus and working smarter all day long.* New York: Harper Collins.
30. https://www.forbes.com/sites/jackzenger/2017/08/17/listening-and-speaking-the-leaders-paradox/#788a11252fff

31. Daimler, M. (2016, May). *Listening is an overlooked leadership tool.* Harvard Business Review. Retrieved from https://hbr.org/2016/05/listening-is-an-overlooked-leadership-tool

32. Goleman, D. *Emotional intelligence: why it can matter more than I Q.* Bloomsbury

33. ATD (August 2018). Lifelong learning—the path to personal and organizational performance. ATD Press.

34. Hougaard, R., & Carter, J. (2018). *The mind of the leader: how to lead yourself, your people, and your organization for extraordinary results.* Boston, MA: Harvard Business Review Press.

35. Neff, K. Retrieved from http://self-compassion.org/the-three-elements-of-self-compassion-2/

36. Goleman, D. *Emotional intelligence: why it can matter more than I Q.* Bloomsbury.

37. University of Michigan—https://positiveorgs.bus.umich.edu/articles/compassion-in-organizational-life/

38. Armstrong, K. (2011). *Twelve steps to a compassionate life.* New York: Anchor Books. Also see her TED Talk.

39. Gladis, S. & Gladis, K. (August, 2018). Prepared for success. TD Magazine.

40. Gladis, S. (2016). *Smile. Breathe. Listen.: The 3 Mindful Acts for Leaders.* Fairfax, VA: SGLP

41. Edmondson, A. C. (2013). *Teaming: how organizations learn, innovate, and compete in the knowledge economy.* San Francisco: Jossey Bass.

42. re:Work - Great managers still matter: the evolution of Google's Project Oxygen. Retrieved from https://rework.withgoogle.com/blog/the-evolution-of-project-oxygen/

43. re:Work. Retrieved from https://rework.withgoogle.com/print/guides/5721312655835136/

44. Edmondson, A. C. (2013). *Teaming: how organizations learn, innovate, and compete in the knowledge economy.* San Francisco: Jossey Bass

45. Brown, B. (2015). *Daring greatly: how the courage to be vulnerable transforms the way we live, love, parent, and lead.* London: Penguin Life.

46. Emotional and Physical Pain Activate Similar Brain Regions. Retrieved from https://www.psychologytoday.com/us/blog/body-sense/201204/emotional-and-physical-pain-activate-similar-brain-regions

47. Brown, B. Transcript of "Listening to shame." Retrieved from https://www.ted.com/talks/brene_brown_listening_to_shame/transcript?language=en

48. Sinek, S. (2019). *Leaders eat last: why some teams pull together and others don't.* London: Penguin Business.

49. Ibid.

50. Rath, T., & Conchie, B. (2009). *Strengths based leadership: great leaders, teams, and why people follow.* New York: Gallup Press.

51. Karlgaard, R. and Malone, M. (2015). *Team genius: the new science of high-performing operations.* Harper Collins.

52. Sinek, S. (2019). *Leaders eat last: why some teams pull together and others don't.* London: Penguin Business.

53. Lieberman, M. (2015). *Social: why our brains are wired to connect.* Oxford University Press.

54. Rheem, D. (2017). *Thrive by design: the neuroscience that drives high-performance cultures.* Charleston, SC: ForbesBooks.

55. Leon Festinger Stanley Schachter and Kurt Back 1950 tracked friendship: Course Hero. Retrieved from https://www.coursehero.com/file/p19igq1/Leon-Festinger-Stanley-Schachter-and-Kurt-Back-1950-tracked-friendship/

56. What is Action Learning? World Institute for Action Learning. Retrieved from https://wial.org/action-learning/

57. Viscott, D. (2003). *Finding your strength in difficult times: a book of meditations.* New York: McGraw-Hill.

58. Amabile, T. M., & Kramer, S. (2011). *The progress principle: using small wins to ignite joy, engagement, and creativity at work.* Boston, MA: Harvard Business Review Press.

59. Rath, T. (2015). *Are You Fully Charged?: The 3 Keys to Energizing Your Work and Life.* United States: Missionday, LLC.

60. Hill, L. A., Brandeau, G., Truelove, E., & Lineback, K. (2014). *Collective genius: the art and practice of leading innovation.* Boston, MA: Harvard Business Review Press.

61. Coyle, D. (2010). *The talent code: Greatness isn't born. It's grown.* London: Arrow.
62. Christensen, C. M., Allworth, J., & Dillon, K. (2019). *How will you measure your life?* London: Thorsons.
63. McCord, P. (2017). *Powerful: building a culture of freedom and responsibility: from the co-creator of Netflix culture deck.* S. l.: Silicon Guild.)
64. Talks, T. E. D., & Steger, M. (2013, March 14). What Makes Life Meaningful: Michael Steger at TEDxCSU. Retrieved from https://www.youtube.com/watch?v=RLFVoEF2RI0
65. (2015, March 19). Having a purpose in life may improve health of aging brain. Retrieved from https://newsarchive.heart.org/having-a-purpose-in-life-may-improve-health-of-aging-brain/
66. Ibid.
67. King, L. What makes life meaningful? Retrieved from https://www.youtube.com/watch?v=vGFJTP_MDO0&feature=youtu.be.
68. Sinek, S., Mead, D., & Docker, P. (2017). *Find your why a practical guide to discovering purpose for you or your team.* New York: Portfolio/Penguin.
69. Wageman, R. (2008). *Senior leadership teams: what it takes to make them great.* Boston, MA: Harvard Business School Press.
70. Doran, G. T. (1981). "There's a S.M.A.R.T. way to write management's goals and objectives". Management Review. 70 (11): 35–36.
71. Wageman, R. (2008). *Senior leadership teams: what it takes to make them great.* Boston, MA: Harvard Business School Press.

Made in the USA
Monee, IL
18 January 2023